The
  Legend
    of
La Llorona

The
Legend
of
La Llorona

Ray John de Aragón

SUNSTONE
PRESS

SANTA FE

Cover and text illustrations by Rosa María Calles

Sunstone books may be purchased for educational, business, or sales promotional use.
For information please write: Special Markets Department, Sunstone Press,
P.O. Box 2321, Santa Fe, New Mexico 87504-2321.

Library of Congress Cataloging-in-Publication Data:

De Aragon, Ray John.
  The legend of La Llorona / Ray John de Aragon.
    p. cm.
  Originally published: Las Vegas, N.M. : Pan American Pub. Co., c1980.
  ISBN 0-86534-505-8 (softcover : alk. paper)
  1. Llorona (Legendary character) 2. Legends--Latin America. I. Title.

GR114.D4 2006
398.20979'02--dc22

                                        2006017893

Published in

WWW.SUNSTONEPRESS.COM
SUNSTONE PRESS/POST OFFICE BOX 2321/SANTA FE, NM 87504-2321/USA
(505) 988-4418/ORDERS ONLY (800) 243-5644/FAX (505) 988-1025

". . . beware the presence of La Llorona
if you dare to read her story. . ."

"Llorando la ausencia
de sus amados hijos
La halla la luna
Y la deja el sol;
Añadiendo siempre
Pasión a pasión,
Memoria a memoria
Dolor a dolor."

"Crying for the absence
of her beloved children
The moon finds her
And the sun leaves her;
Adding always
Passion to passion
Memory to memory
Pain to pain."

I

INTRODUCTION TO LA LLORONA

here are certain legends that exist throughout the world which appear to have come from man's overpowering fear of the unknown. Tales of superstition can be found in all cultures. They are steeped in mystery. All such tales have the common bond of an encounter with the forces of the supernatural. One can still trace these stories of darkness and forbidding appearances in musty worm eaten manuscripts. A spine-tingling account of a crying, wandering spirit of a woman was written down centuries ago. It became a popular legend in Spanish America, although the original documents were lost in the sands of time.

The legend appeared from a time in which belief in witchcraft was at a peak. Witch trials and burnings were a common occurrence. It was generally believed, some people possessed magic and mystical powers inherited from the Devil. With these powers they could play havoc with mankind during their lives and after death.

The Spanish colonists of the sixteenth century called the other-worldly spirits that return, "*Almas que andan penando*, (souls in search of peace)." It was said, these poor lost souls had suffered a terrible death during their wretched lives. The tormented spirits had thus been cast unto eternal damnation. The spirits had been forced to go out in search of peace. A peace which could only be attained by having their ghostly apparitions laid to rest. La Llorona, a tormented spirit in search of peace, wanders over all of the earth. The people pray to redeem her wandering soul. The priests chant requiem hymns over the graves of those possessed by her and exorcise those still living that have seen her.

The story of La Llorona is now a classic legend. Having survived in Spanish folklore for more than four centuries, it remains as popular today as when the events were reported to have taken place. A cult has grown in Teotihuacan, Southern Mexico, and Honduras in a half reverance, half idealism of La Llorona. Those that take part in recalling her spirit, sing a ritual song in her honor. The chief singer is usually a young man that sings for her to appear to him as the extraordinarily beautiful woman she was during life. He sings of a mystic love that he has for La Llorona and longs to fulfill his desires for her by seeing her spirit. Many claim to have seen the wailing woman and say they were captivated by her strange magnetic beauty. They long to be taken by her to live in what they think would be an eternal bliss.

Stories are currently circulated in many Latin American cities, including La Paz, Bolivia, of possible sightings of La Llorona. Certain newspapers are known to carry sensationalized reports of unexplained deaths being related to her treacherous spirit. When a youth or elder suffers an unusually severe heart attack late at night, the wailing woman is immediately blamed for yet another homicide. Therefore, tales continue to multiply and the legend thrives.

Variations of the legend exist in the folklore of other world cultures. In the Scandinavian countries she is known as the beautiful lady in white that beckons unsuspecting victims to death. It is claimed that once one has seen her, she overcomes all of our human emotions to claim our souls. In the state and city of Oaxaca, Mexico, La Llorona is also described as a beautiful young woman dressed in white. Her mournful wail can be heard late at night because she is filled with regret at having murdered her children.

French folklore is full of stories centered around the Lady who haunts the moor. She is depicted as an evil spirit, "dressed all in flowing white and her teeth as having become very long." Her sad wailing can be heard in the haunting winds of night as she leads travelers to their untimely deaths in the moor.

A folktale which originated in Dahomey and Togoland in Africa was introduced to the United States by Black Americans who were brought to America as slaves. As an oral story which changed in the retelling, it describes the wind as a wailing woman that roams the waterways in search of her murdered children. They were drowned by the ocean, who is also a woman, and scattered throughout the world. The wind fights desperately with the water trying to retrieve her lost children.

Washington Irving himself in his famous Legend of Sleepy Hollow mentions an early Dutch tale about a woman in white. As a chronicler of the Dutch settlements on the Eastern seaboard of the United States, Irving was especially attracted to the folklore and legends of the Dutch colonists. A popular story centered around an old tree where "cries and wailings could be heard." A woman in white was reported to haunt the area near the tree in the dark glen at Raven Rock. She was, "heard to shriek on winter nights."

The symbolic form of the weeping woman is found in Gaelic folklore. Known as the "banshee," pronounced, "bansidhe," she is a supernatural being whose mournful wailing is said to foretell death. Like other creatures of European folklore, the banshee has crossed the Atlantic from Ireland into America.

In ancient American Indian mythology one can find accounts of a weeping woman of death in search of her loved ones. The Aztecs themselves related the story of Ciuacoatl a weeping goddess, in their ancient myths. She would capture infants from their cradles, and after killing them would roam the streets of Tenochtitlan at night with a mournful wail, foreshadowing wars and misery.

The Mexican goddess always appeared in white. Her sinister face was painted half red and half black. She wore a feather headdress, golden earplugs and carried a turquoise weaving stick. Tales of Ciuacoatl, as those of other Aztec gods and goddesses, come from preceding versions borrowed from the civilization of the Mayas. It is now believed by learned scholars the stories predate the Maya culture and actually stem from a much earlier race.

In Seville and other areas of Spain there are stories which resemble those of the now popular Spanish American legend of La Llorona. It can be stated, with some degree of certainty, that La Llorona is a universal legend. She may be known by different names, but there are striking similarities between one version and another. Stories of La Llorona, in some instances, also bear a strong resemblance to those of the Angel of Death which stem from fourteenth century Europe. Whenever her tragic spirit is seen, death is assuredly near. She sometimes appears dressed in black and has long hair and long fingernails. Her face is that of a skeleton and she travels surrounded by a white mist.

People have believed in stories similar to La Llorona all over the world since the earliest recorded times. The legend itself through variations reaches back many centuries before Christ to ancient Rome and Greece.

In ancient Greek mythology we find the story of Ino, which resembles those of La Llorona. According to the legend, Athamas, king of the prehistoric Minyans in the ancient Boeotian city of Orchomenus, falls in love with Ino, the daughter of Cadmus. He neglects his own wife Nephele, a cloud goddess. Nephele disappears in anger.

Athamas and Ino have two sons, Learchus and Melicertes. Ino also nurses the god Dionysus. This incurs the wrath of Hera, wife of Zeus. According to Euripedes, an early Greek poet born in 480 B.C., Hera drives Ino mad. Ino then kills herself and her two children together. The story of Ino varies even in Greek legend. She is later worshipped by the early Greeks as Leucothea, the White Goddess.

Euripedes, the last of the three great ancient Greek tragedians, takes up the myth of Ino and incorporates it into his famous play, Medea. In this version, Medea is an enchantress who helps Jason, leader of the Argonauts, to obtain the Golden Fleece from her father, King Aeetes of Colchis. Medea is later married to Jason and she uses her magical powers to help him.

Jason and Medea give birth to two sons. He, however, decides to abandon Medea in favor of marrying a Greek princess, Creusa, the daughter of Creon, King of Corinth. In the play of Medea, presented in 431 B.C., she murders her two children in despair. Medea is subdued with sorrow saying,

> "Ah! Ah! Stop, my heart. Do not you commit this crime. Leave them alone, unhappy one, spare the children. Even if they live far from us, they will bring you joy. No! By the unforgettable dead in hell, it cannot be! I shall not leave my children for my enemies to insult. (In any case they must die. And if die they must, I shall slay them, who gave them birth.)"

Medea murders her children, leaving everyone horrified with her crime. Her deed goes unpunished. She escapes in a dragon chariot. Medea takes refuge with King Aegeus of Athens. The Greek historian, Herodotus related that from Athens Medea went to Media. Medea herself became the Dragon Queen of Media. At last she is represented as becoming immortal and marrying Achilles in the underworld.

Ovid in his Metamorphoses carried the story of Medea further. Publius Ovidius Naso was a Roman poet born on March 20 in 43 B.C. at Sulmo (modern Sulmona). Ovid wrote a tragedy based on Medea which was, in time, lost. We know that it was praised by the critic Quintilian and the historian Tacitus. Ovid's Medea eventually influenced Seneca, who wrote another play on the same theme.

Lucius Annaeus Seneca was an Hispano-Roman tragedian born about 4 B.C. at Corduba (Cordoba). His thought became a component of the Latin culture of the Middle Ages.

MEDEA

As the first of the truly "Spanish" thinkers, his influence in Spain was always powerful.

Ancient accounts of Medea describe her as having had a profound knowledge of the magical virtues of plants and practicing witchcraft. Aeschylus and Sophocles used her as a subject in their tragedies and Quintus Ennius took the theme for one of his works.

An ancient painting of Medea has been discovered which has been attributed to Aristolaus Timomachus. Eugene Delacroix portrayed the malevolent Medea in two of his famous classical works. As a singular subject or as a subject of larger compositions, Medea has played a role in numerous artistic representations of the classical period.

The story of Medea was dramatized by Pierre Corneille, a French dramatist often called "the father of French tragedy," in 1635; Luigi Cherubini, Italian composer, in 1797, and Franz Grillparzer, Austrian dramatist in 1821. Grillparzer presented Jason and Medea with marital and cultural problems which ended in bitter disillusionment and resignation. Similarities between the presentation of Medea and the theme of La Llorona are too closely related to be dismissed as mere coincidence.

According to legend, Jason was a prince of Iolcus, an ancient city in Thessaly, Northeastern Greece near modern Volas. He sailed in his ship, Argo, to search for a mythical Golden Fleece. Jason and his Argonauts, those who sailed with him on his ship, traveled to Colchis, a region of the western Georgian Soviet Socialist Republics, in search of the fleece. It was here that he met Medea.

In Maikop, 56 miles east of the Black Sea, which is near Colchis, archaeologists have made a striking discovery. A version of the story of Jason and the Argonauts was found inscribed on an ancient stone. Scholars have identified the writing as Phoenician and have dated it between the 12th and 8th centuries B.C. The Phoenicians themselves later settled on the Iberian Peninsula (Spain). It is now believed this discovery confirms that the Greek legend of Jason and the Argonauts and possibly Medea is apparently true.

Some writers that have gathered stories of La Llorona tend to associate its origins as stemming directly from American Indian mythology. Still others ascribe to a contemporary

MEDEA . *Eugene Delacroix* . *The Louvre Museum, Paris*

belief which states tales of La Llorona were derived from the actual life of La Malinche. A story has been woven which declares La Malinche, an Indian princess who aided Cortez in his conquest of the Aztec empire, betrayed her people. She became an outcast, produced two illegitimate children fathered by Cortez and spent the remainder of her short life plagued by remorse over her traitorous act. Unaccepted and denounced by Indian and Spaniard alike, La Malinche is pictured as a torn wailing woman forever punished for her foresaking deed.

In truth, La Malinche, or Malinali, was a member of the distinct tribe of Indians of Coatzacoalcos. This group never came under the subjugation of Montezuma and his Aztecs. She was indeed the mother of a child fathered by Cortez, but later on became the wife of Juan Jaramillo. She bore him a daughter and according to Bernal Diaz del Castillo lived out the rest of her life with her family. Having become a Christian, she was buried in the church of the Holy Trinity.

Since many of the tribes of mesoamerica hated the Aztecs including those that allied themselves with Cortez to defeat the empire, La Malinche was not regarded as a perfidious woman. Although not an Aztec, La Malinche was highly respected by them before and after the conquest. She received the reverential name of Malintzin. In true life she was admired by both Indian and Spaniard. Although it is difficult to separate fact from myth in reference to La Malinche, one thing is certain: she never regretted aiding Cortez in the defeat of the Aztec empire nor was she rejected by the Indians because of it. Also, she was never filled with hopeless anguish caused by a sense of guilt from being the mother of an illegitimate child.

There are many true life stories which could be matched with the versions of La Llorona. Far too numerous to mention here. In fact, so many similar episodes have occurred in the lives of some women that it would be difficult to disclaim a direct connection to the "wailing woman" of legend. However, one must rely upon oral tradition, historical evidence and one significant point found missing in contemporary themes of La Llorona. The essential constituent of the supernatural element that is a basic part of the entire legend is lacking. Also, during the Spanish Middle Ages, La Llorona was already a part of Spanish mythology. Spanish Conquistadores had known about her before encountering the Aztecs and their civilization.

It is my personal belief that a writer during the Spanish Golden Age incorporated the subject of Medea in one of his works. As Medea was already popularized as a fascinating, dangerous siren, this gave rise to the tale of La Llorona with her beckoning wail.

Seneca's story of Medea may very well be the primary source for those of La Llorona. Whatever the case, Medea's or La Llorona's stories could have grown from two distinct but similar events in different periods of history. It is not altogether improbable that like tragedies to those of Medea and La Llorona have occurred throughout the course of time.

After extensive research it now seems certain that the version of La Llorona, which has gained in such widespread popularity, comes to the Southwestern part of the United States from the sixteenth century settlement of the New World by the Spanish. The story apparently spread from the city of Mexico in, as it was called back then, New Spain and traveled throughout the Spanish Empire which included the Netherlands.

The legend of La Llorona has taken dramatic changes through the centuries. Most Spanish speaking communities proudly lay claim to the story as a part of their local folklore. The story was passed on by word of mouth and it received a special touch of flavor from the person retelling it.

The tale would be recounted by early colonists on cold wintry nights while family members gathered near a warm fire place. Storytellers would readily change the names of the principal characters, locations of events, dates and other details of the original story. Many times it was unintentional due to loss of memory. But more often, it was to bring La Llorona closer to home by saying she had been a local girl that had met an untimely death due to the murder of her children. The grandparents of some knew her "personally and were present at her trial and execution for the murders of the children." Therefore, her story was just as vivid to residents of towns in New Mexico, Texas, or California as to those in Cuba, Mexico or Spain.

The legend always involves a love affair between a peasant

girl and a rich man that refuses to marry her for some reason. She gives birth to children out of wedlock and later kills them in despair. Here the stories vary as to how she commits the murders. In Mexico they claim she drowned the children in a well. Stories in the Southwestern United States range from the use of a hatchet, axe or dagger, to drowning in an arroyo or river. She is pictured as a woman torn by a tragic event. Her children are starving and she kills them to save them from their misery, or she kills them to keep them away from their father. Shortly after her death, the sinister spirit of La Llorona was seen rising from the grave. She arose to haunt dark alleys or roam the waterways near villages and towns in a fruitless search for her children. La Llorona was described as an evil spirit that returned to prey upon both the living and the dead. Deep in northern New Mexico, old-timers recall having seen a mysterious flame or ball of fire that is often associated with the appearance of her ghoulish spirit. They not only state her ghost returns, but scenes from her tragic life can reappear as well.

The legend was at times used as a disciplinary tool. Parents or grandparents claimed La Llorona especially seeks the bad children. Upon finding them, she would take the children and they would never be heard from or seen again. The eyes of the little ones open wide as the crackling embers in the fireplace create images of La Llorona in their vivid imaginations. Children listen eagerly to their stories. The braver ones search in desolate arroyos for her spirit by day, but never venture forth by night. With an unexpected noise or moving shadow, they rush home to tell of their narrow escape from the wailing spirit. It must have been through a miracle, they say.

II

THE LEGEND

young, fearless man was out for a night ride on horseback. The solemn night was pitchdark as he rode aimlessly through the winding narrow road. The horses thundering hooves beat out a drum-like tune as they hit the rock laden dirt and kicked up the dust. The moonlight rider gave a self-assured glance as he passed rapidly by the night specters. Owls and hidden predators alike cast knowing looks upon the night intruder.

As the brave horseman reached an open field, a glowing light in the distance caught his attention. Laughter and singing echoed through the brisk wind. He quickly decided to ride toward the bright light. He steadily drew nearer and saw that the questionable light came from a tall building. He cautiously dismounted when he arrived and walked with brisk paces to a near window. Cleaning the soiled pane, he could see a group of merry people dancing and conversing in a large hall. The loud piercing music coming from within made him wonder who could be having a late dance.

He felt uneasy, but his curiousity forced him to enter. He walked unnoticed amidst the mysterious strangers. Their unusual clothing was very peculiar to him. A piercing cold passed through his tense body as he saw the staring eyes of the festive crowd. They appeared to look right through him. An eerie feeling made him desirous of leaving. The night rider left and mounted his waiting horse anxiously wanting to return home.

On his way back through the deserted road an orange flame appeared ahead of him. It became larger and larger with his steady approach. He desperately tried to ride away from it but it seemed to follow him. Suddenly the glowing flame vanished. At the same moment his strong horse reared violently. An elderly woman stood off to his right. His heavy heart pounded. The aged woman's translucent body seemed to float in the night air. It swiftly moved towards him. The tense horse became frightened and took off in a mad gallop.

A strange wailing cry could be heard carried through the cold wind as he rode on. The normally brave rider felt sure it came from the unholy spirit he imagined following him.

At last, he saw a small dwelling which promised to provide refuge from his fears. Sound and motion seemed to slow down as his tired horse agonizingly moved toward the distant house. Once there he jumped off his weary horse not daring to look back. Knocking at the wooden door, the man's strained muscles ached and he found himself gasping for breath. The open space around him seemed to be closing in. He knocked harder. The sheer state of panic caused him to lose all sense of consciousness.

The young man's languid condition made his confused mind wander in wicked reflections of demoniac scenes. Clutching, writhing beings seemed to be pulling him down into the devil's inferno. An odor of burnt ashes seemed to permeate and linger in the chilled air.

The woman appeared with a hideous, mocking laugh. But then her distorted face cracked with lines of sorrow. Her pain filled eyes stressed her inner anguish and her inflamed body became a vision of agony while the fires of hell burnt around her. She reached out to him in a pleading way as if begging for him to help her.

A loud voice interrupted his mental visions. He found himself being rapidly transported through a darkened tunnel. The frightened man strove to reach a faint light at the distant end. His astonished eyes opened to discover a lighted candle. His blurred vision could make out the hazy form of a wooden statue held by a wrinkled hand. The weakened horseman was startled but a reassuring voice calmed him. It was Tía Elena, the village curandera (Healer). She helped him up and took him into her warm home. She knew him as Ricardo Valdez.

Tiá Elena was a small, slender woman. At eighty-six her sharp wit proved the elderly curandera was quite knowledgeable. As she served Ricardo rose petal tea, he spoke of his terrifying experience. The attentive woman sat silently in deep thought as Ricardo recounted the recent events in vivid detail. She made the sign of the cross when he mentioned the translucent spirit and the wailing cry. Tiá Elena's thinned lips parted as she prayed silently. Ricardo failed to notice her worried look as he clearly described the odd clothing of the occult dancers.

The youthful man's voice quivered at times as he spoke to the esteemed curandera. His excitement made him seem quite unlike the fearless man he formerly made himself out to be. As Ricardo came to the end of his unbelieveable story he caught the elderly woman in a total state of meditation. He could not fully understand why tears suddenly appeared from her weathered old eyes. She began to respond after he called out to her several times.

Tiá Elena explained,

"You saw La Llorona. The wailing woman that appeared to you is a tormented soul. No one has ever found the key to help her ease her heart breaking agony. She is still in search of peace. She longs to be laid to rest. I have heard her mournful cry in the haunting wind. Our forefathers grieved for her and prayed for her repentance, yet she still returns in a desperate search. Some say it is a never ending search for her two children."

"Yes, but what does all this have to do with me? I have heard countless stories of La Llorona before, but I always felt that it was a fantasy or at best a storytellers nonsense,"

Ricardo answered.

"Ah, my son you may have been chosen to see her pathetic vision because of your skepticism. I can only share my experience with you. First you must open your heart and mind to things which are unknown, then you shall be wiser. In your case, the Evil One has taken the first step in claiming your soul. You must do something or you will sicken and die."

Upon hearing this Ricardo's reaction was one of disbelief. He objected strenuously to the aged woman.

"If what you say is true, how is it that such a thing could happen to me?"

She replied,

"Once someone has seen her spellbinding spirit, La Llorona overcomes all of that person's human emotions to claim the soul. This has happened to many before you and they have all died."

19

Ricardo then implored,

"What can I do to save myself?"

Tía Elena advised the agitated man,

"It seems there is but one thing you can possibly do. Help La Llorona find peace. Then she may be able to release you from her grasp and her death beckoning powers shall cease. There may be a written record of her life wherein your answer may lie. Perhaps Fray Carlos at the church can help you."

The loud crowing of the roosters signaled the beginning of a new day. Ricardo and the wise curandera had spent the remainder of the memorable night conversing about the wailing woman of death. She offered him a bowl of warm blue corn meal (atole). Ricardo thankfully accepted. Tía Elena reached into a low drawer of a large aged and darkened cupboard and pulled something out.

"I am going to give you a religious medallion of Santa Rita. She is the saint that grants the impossible. Perhaps if you wear it and pray to her she will intercede in your behalf."

Ricardo was overjoyed with the bronze medal and tied the string it hung from around his neck. He embraced the elderly woman as he thanked her for her gracious help. The curandera blessed Ricardo saying, "I will pray to all the saints for your soul." He mounted his horse, and after riding away glanced back to see her waving.

The bright clear sunny day filled him with a new source of inner strength. Tía Elena's words continued to plague him as he thought about the possibility of dying.

"Could she have been mistaken?"
He wondered.

As Ricardo thought more about the mind shattering events of the previous night and the curandera's advice, he decided to retrace his tracks. The winding trail was easy to follow. He was in extreme need of an answer. Could he find it by returning to the scene of the dancing crowd?

Ricardo pulled tightly on the reins of his horse as he came to an abrupt stop. He sat stupified and motionless staring directly ahead of him. The night terror he had experienced was recreated in his mind. He hesitated for an infinite moment but once again dismounted and walked to the window. The building itself was nothing more than ruins of a large, once proud dwelling in sorrowful decay.

Ricardo reached the darkened window. The pane was scraped clean as he himself had left it. He soon learned the shocking truth. As he looked into the spacious room he could see that everything was covered with dirt. Broken furniture lay about at random. It was clear the place had been in a state of disuse for a long length of time.

Storm clouds were brewing and the weather strangely changed. Ricardo felt an unearthly presence. Whether or not it was imaginary, he did not care to find out. He quickly left. As the frightened young man rode home he thought worriedly of how he could explain his long absence to his family. His parents, he knew, would have waited up for him the entire night.

Ricardo lived in the old city of Santa Fe in New Mexico. It was a quiet, peaceful village nestled near the beautiful and majestic Sangre de Cristo Mountains. The early Spanish settlers had set up the village which served as the capital for the government of the northern frontier of New Spain. The colonists had arrived with both their religion and superstitions. Witchcraft was practiced by known and feared brujas (witches) whereas curanderas were sought to cure evil spells.

The sky grew steadily blacker as the rain swollen clouds met and formed a heavy blanket over Santa Fe. Ricardo's uneasiness went rampant as his imagination took over his senses. He knew he would have to take the curander's advice. It seemed to be an omen of impending doom. His doom!

Ricardo met his anxious parents, younger sister and brother gathered in the living room. Alberto Valdez was quite angry at what he thought was his son's carelessness.

The uneasy young man explained what had happened. His younger brother and sister were excited and thoroughly interested in the strange story. Their parents, however, took the possible sighting of La Llorona quite seriously.

"I wish I could have seen her," his younger brother, Tomas, spoke out. Their devoted mother interrupted before he could go on.

"Tía Elena is highly regarded. A curandera's advice should not go unheeded. A very close friend of mine, Maria, perished after seeing La Llorona. Tomas, you do not understand how serious this is,"

his mother tearfully stated. Their father also agreed,

"Ricardo, you must lose no time in searching out Fray Carlos. Even if you honestly believe it is more of a nightmare than reality, please do it for your mother's sake. Remember your nana's (grandmother's) favorite saying, 'Dios les ayuda a los que se ayudan', (God helps those that help themselves). Through helping yourself find an answer you will relieve any doubt from your mind."

Finally convinced by his parents wise reasoning, Ricardo decided in favor of discussing the mystifying enigma with the friar.

"May God by with you," they pronounced in unison as he asked their leave and quickly stepped out the door. Certainly no one could readily predict what would be Fray Carlos' response. Ricardo, in any case, felt assured that as a man of the cloth, the friar could provide the solution and if need be, the protection he desired.

Ricardo walked nervously towards the San Miguel church. Suddenly his mind was preoccupied with the curandera's warning after seeing a nauseating hearse. It was carting off a victim of sword wounds to the mortuary. The curious man glanced at the opened cart. The rigid corpse seemed to stare back coldly as if giving Ricardo the kiss of death. Terrified he advanced hurriedly to the church to see the friar.

Fray Carlos Delgado had recently been assigned on temporary duty to the parish of Santa Fe. He already had more than thirty five years of service in New Mexico and now preferred the more serene atmosphere of the San Miguel church. The building itself had a pyramidal three-storied tower. There were almenas or adobe crenellations around its roof. The crenellated parapet served as a reminder that the church was responsible for both the salvation of souls and human lives when warring Indian tribes attacked unexpectedly.

In the interior Fray Carlos often enjoyed seeing the painted wooden altar screen. The detailed work was done by the famed Laguna santero. Its floral elements, framing canvasses from New Spain and the patron's statue, were of soft coral pink and sage green. The paintings on buffalo hides which hung on the massive walls were the only dismal touch to the otherwise friendly surroundings. The painting of San Sebastian gruesomely protrayed the martyred saint pierced with arrows. The blood and agony were overemphacized to cause horror in the minds of the shocked viewers.

The artwork was not a pretty sight for Ricardo as he entered the ponderous church. He exited through a side door after being informed the fray was out working in the church gardens. The inexperienced man found Fray Carlos tending to the grape vines in the patio. The thin wiry fray joyfully sang as he moved from plant to plant. The prudent friar was recognized by all as being well versed in mysterious things. He had a worn weathered look which made it clear he had an austere dedication of ministering on the merciless frontier.

After greeting young Valdez with a friendly smile and an assuring statement, Fray Carlos led him into the comfortable rectory to sit. The kind friar listened very attentively to his apparently serious problem. Ricardo asked as he came to the end.

"Can it really be the wrath of La Llorona
as I have been told father?"

Noticing the man's near hysteria the sensitive friar wisely answered,

"Listen my son, you have no need to worry. You are a faithful Christian and closely follow the teachings of our Savior. An evil spirit will not claim your soul."

"I believe what you say is true father, but I did not imagine what happened last night. I feel deeply troubled by an experience I cannot explain logically."

The concerned priest sought to counsel Ricardo by considering the matter with an open mind. He reasoned,

"There is nothing more to fear than fear itself. The mind can at times play many illogical tricks with our imagination. If we

24

allow our psyche to be dominated by its abili-
ty to elaborate erratic or bizarre images, then
we can no longer see clearly. Vile fantasy is
suddenly transformed into vexing reality.
Besides, we have more to fear from the living
than from those who are dead."

Fray Carlos Delgado blessed Ricardo as he excused himself
from the meeting to say his evening Mass.

"If you should need me again please come
and I will do anything within my power to
help you,"

the friar stated.

"I shall dedicate this Mass for you."

"Thank you, father," young Valdez responded as he bid
the fray farewell. He walked silently into the crowded church
to sit amongst the other people in the pews to attend the
Mass.

He felt genuine relief from the friar's comforting words.
But the disturbing events were still too close to memory to be
dismissed so quickly. The troubled eyes of the luminous spirit
he had seen were firmly planted in his subconscious. Leaving
the church in the dark of night rapidly subdued his efforts to
do away with supernatural thoughts.

Before Ricardo lay back to sleep that windy night, he lit a
small candle before his patron saint. The resulting shadows
began to create unpleasant thoughts for him. The spent wick
flickered and the dark shadows moved uncomfortably about
the windowless room. Ricardo tried to brush away the
resulting images by immersing his burdened mind in prayer.
Not succeeding he arose from his low wooden bed and put
out the disturbing light. Returning to his bed he nervously
toyed with the idea of death. La Llorona came to mind and at
times she even seemed to overpower him with an intense
desire to seek the hereafter.

It was near mid-morning before Ricardo finally dozed off.
His nightmarish dreams recreated the horrifying events of the
past few days. Tía Elena appeared as well as Fray Carlos. But
as Ricardo came to the end of his dream he saw himself walking through a thick mist. As the mist cleared he saw the morbid tombstones of a rural cemetery. He subconsciously pulled
away but a powerful mental force kept him walking past the

gloomy sepulchers to a predetermined stone. There he shockingly saw his name chiseled into the marker. Seeing the date of his death he awakened with terrifying screams. Ricardo's parents rushed into his room finding him shaking in utter fear.

Ricardo Valdez lost no time in returning to the friar for help. This time Fray Delgado saw he was very emphatic about his inner mental anguish. The priest offered a possible solution to the problem which involved an exorcism. Thusly it was reasoned the afflicted man would be free of an evil spirit, if such were the case. But the friar stressed the point that such a decision would have to be made by his superior in Mexico. An investigation would have to be held. The determination could take months before it were received back in Santa Fe.

In desperation Ricardo contended he could not endure the hardship of waiting for an answer to his frightful plague. Recalling the curandera's advice of finding a written record wherein the key could be found, Valdez asked for the friar's assistance.

> "Perhaps," the fray responded, "you could find a written clue which may place your mind at ease."

Realizing the power of inducing a belief, the friar placed more credence to the curandera's opinion. He went on to relate,

> "I did extensive study in my early days at the monasteries in Mexico. I recall visiting one monastery in particular which housed all of the written records of the Franciscan friars. The old monastery of San Sebastian, of which I speak, lies a few miles south of the City of Mexico. I once entered a large vault which contained an immense store of knowledge accumulated since the year 1551. Every type and description of recorded learning from the time of the conquest onward can be found on the handwritten journals. Perhaps you might find your desired information there."

Ricardo Valdez now had a definite goal to reach. Now there was a thread of hope. After discovering from the helpful friar how to reach San Sebastian, Ricardo lost no time in preparing for his demanded journey. Although his parents feared for his safety, they agreed no time could be lost. They, more than anyone else, could see a radical change in their beloved son's behavior. It was the dead of winter when he joined a group of religious penitent pilgrims traveling South together in a caravan to Mexico. They were on their way to see the revered cloak of Juan Diego which contained the miraculous printed image of Our Lady of Guadalupe.

The constant vision of the wailing woman's sorrow filled eyes could not be erased from Ricardo's mind during the gloomy darkness of the endless nights. She would appear as an evil spirit attempting to suffocate him in his sleep. The despairing man continued suffering from fantastic nightmares. His hallucinations made him feel certain he was at death's door as the slow moving caravan made its way through a deserted region. The area had been named La Jornada de la Muerte (The Journey of Death) by the Conquistadores. The timeless excursion was filled with an enduring hardship which made it seem like he would never find the answer to his frightful plague.

Ricardo finally did arrive at the ancient monastery known as San Sebastian, in the midst of an unusually harsh storm. The like of which had never before been experienced so far south into Mexico. It was attributed to an unexplained phenomena associated with the sun. All feared the end of the world was at hand. The puzzled monks could scarcely believe their eyes as they saw Ricardo standing there looking with glazed eyes, not at all unlike a specter himself. His long hair and beard were encrusted with particles of snow that had become frozen where they lay. The brothers helped him into a warm room and seated him near the fireplace. Ricardo's feet were nearly frostbitten. His teeth chattered as he tried to explain the reason for his arrival. Being quite incoherent to the bewildered friars, Ricardo removed a folded letter written by Fray Carlos to the superior at the monastery.

Fray Alonso Benavidez arrived after being advised of the strange visitor's presence. He was given the informative message immediately. Placing his square rimmed spectacles to his eyes he read the message silently. With the unusual information contained on the page he could now explain to the others the purpose of the stranger's untimely visit. Ricardo was given nourishment by the kindly friars and led to a warm bed. It would take several days of rest to recuperate to the point of conversing with the superior.

Fray Benavidez tapped loudly at the guest room door as Ricardo was finishing the final morsels of his evening meal. The curious host wished to hear every stirring detail of Valdez' trying adventure. Ricardo's mind was reawakened as he vividly described the mystifying events. He often appeared on the verge of a mental breakdown as he emotionally stated he was near death. Finally, regaining his composure, the desperate man pleaded for help. Fray Alonso's answer had a calmative effect.

> "Your experience does pose an interesting problem. You can rest assured we will be of service and assist you in any way possible. Please feel free to ask for anything you need at anytime, day or night. God works in very mysterious ways. If you have actually been chosen to lay a wandering soul to rest, you should consider yourself in a very special way. As you know, we help the poor souls in Purgatory through our merciful prayers. We can intercede here on Earth for those who have died impenitent by our own good deeds and sacrifices done on their behalf. Perhaps this particular soul you speak of is undergoing unrelenting suffering, and atonement for her sins is especially demanding."

The benevolent priest blessed the young man. Ricardo smiled and thanked him for his gracious help.

In a matter of days, Ricardo felt physically well enough to begin his research. He was led into the stabbing chill of the vault where the registers from remote antiquity were kept. Asking to be left alone, Ricardo settled down at an old table with a large group of documents to begin his time consuming venture. He now hoped he could prove whether his experience was real or only an erratic figment of the imagination.

Day after day the lone researcher examined numerous manuscripts, registers and single papers in a fruitless search. He would go at times without eating and his physical health deteriorated. The distressed frays attempted to help Ricardo.

They begged him to care for his well being but the search became a mad obsession.

"It must be here!"
he yelled. Flipping the yellowed pages frantically it appeared that Ricardo had lost all reason.

"I'll find the damn story of La Llorona if
it's the last thing I do!" He told Fray Alonso.

"It may be the last thing you do if you continue at the same rate as you are now doing!"
answered the fray. The compassionate priest was very concerned for him but Ricardo did not care to listen. He pushed the fray violently as he forced him to leave the dreary vault.

The tormented man was losing all hope of finding anything about the wailing woman. He sat down and cried uncontrollably as he pictured himself closer to the summoning grave. He was exhausted and beaten. Looking about the sullen room he noticed a group of dusty papers on an almost hidden shelf he had apparently missed. He felt himself strangely drawn to them. He genuinely began thinking there was still a chance. Ricardo rushed and picked up the yellowed documents with trembling fingers. He laid the crumbling papers out under the glowing candle light to read them. The opening lines were almost illegible. But, as the wind moaned eerily beyond the cracked walls of the silent chamber, Ricardo alarmingly made out the blurred words,

"La Llorona se llevo a la niña, Veronica,
(The wailing woman took the child,
Veronica)."

Ricardo heard a wolf's doleful howl in the distance. He nervously read on,

"Beware the presence of La Llorona if you
dare to read her story."

To Ricardo the warning was of no significance. It was a question of life or death. The ancient account continued.

"I, Fray Benedicto de la Prada, of the
church of San Geronimo, on the 18th day of
May in the year of our Lord, 1642, being
asked to exorcise the child, Veronica, have so
done. I was, regretfully, too late in the perfor-
mance of this solemn rite. When I was sum-
moned to deliver the sacred ritual, I sor-

rowfully found the poor child in a state of dementia. She had strayed away from her home one black night without her parents knowledge. The terrified parents were hysterical when they could not find the girl in her bedroom. They employed the help of neighbors to search for her. Everyone heard Veronica's deafening screams and madly sought to reach her. They then saw La Llorona's phantom withdraw as the spreading light of the metal lanterns illuminated the thickened forest. I anointed Veronica with Holy Oils, but her possessed soul has now been lost to the wailing woman forever . . .

"The honorable prefect of this villa prayed that I give him a full account of the life of Lusia Gertrudis de Panuelo, who is popularly known as La Llorona. I am complying with the request being that it is my wish to help in having her tortured soul find peace. The astounding story was given to one of my predecessors through the vow of the secrecy of the confessional. It was recorded in the old priest's diary for reference of future curates of the church. The diary was later encased in a coffer and sealed in the wall of the vestry. No one other than the prefect is to read it, for it is now said that a curse follows it. I shall deliver the necessary exorcism when it is returned."

Ricardo came to the end of the water stained page and carefully turned it to the next. He was full of anticipation as his searching eyes strained to decipher the ancient writing. Ricardo's burning desire to learn more came to a abrupt end as page after page contained only brief accounts of Baptisms, marriages, and deaths. Was this the end of his search for La Llorona? He painstakingly went over the church registers many times in a vain effort to learn more. A certain passage caught Ricardo's attention.

"The diary was encased in a coffer and sealed in the wall of the vestry."

Ricardo left quickly and went to seek out Fray Alonso for more information. He found the elderly priest meditating in the brightly lit chapel. The unthinking young man dashed into the silent room and surprised the fray with a barrage of questions. Ricardo was terribly excited but the patient friar finally calmed him down. Young Valdez explained what he had found.

"As I was searching for a sign, any sign that would lead me to an answer, I found an old church register with a curious message. It pertained to an exorcism officiated by the pastor of the San Geronimo mission. The demoniac takeover of an innocent soul was attributed to La Llorona. The precise pastor made mention of a diary wherein the tormented spirit's entire story was written down. He described in detail the prized diary was placed for safekeeping in a wall of the church. Could the diary still be there after all of these centuries?"

Ricardo asked. Fray Alonso stated,

"The San Geronimo church is located on the outskirts of the village. It is a dreary building which is in intense decay. It was abandoned during the seventeenth century after the pastor was found dead under mysterious circumstances. The townspeople refused to go near it. The massive structure then fell into rapid disuse. Some people swore they could hear unearthly laughter and screams coming from within at midnight. As far as any diary being sealed in the vestry is concerned, I cannot answer one way or the other."

Ricardo declared,

"Then I must go there and find out for myself!"

The fray again insisted,

"Ricardo, you should look after your health. If you must go off in a search for more answers, wait and do so in the morning."

But Ricardo had to find the needed diary. He argued intensely,

"My health is failing me to such an extent
that I fear I will not live past another day."

The mental torment he had been experiencing at times made him ramble in his speech. The friars in turn now feared him as a man on the verge of madness. Ricardo flew past the horrified friars and out the door unopposed, grasping the lantern he had been using in the vault.

A bright full moon made it quite easy for the troubled young man to find his way. The silvery orb played a game with him as it danced in and out from between the towering trees. A swift breeze rustled the leaves and they made a scratchy noise. The scene reminded Ricardo of a song from the dark recesses of his mind called *The Dance of The Goblins*. The appalling shadows of the night threateningly followed him as he neared the church cemetery. A soft blanket of gloomy mist suddenly came over the sepulchers which led the path to the doorway.

Monument stones lay strewn as though they had been pushed aside by a powerful force. Some still remained standing and they loomed high as sentinels of the dead. He heard a mournful cry. Ricardo stopped and saw two large eyes staring at him. An unholy feeling made Ricardo shudder with fear as he drew steadily nearer. As he strained his eyes he could make out the outline of an owl. Ricardo broke out in a reassuring laughter inspite of his inner anguish. He moved on to the dominant church.

There he stood before the heavy hand chiseled doors which blocked his entry. They were richly decorated with strange forbidding medieval creatures, grotesque gargoyles. Ricardo felt they were placed there to remind impenitent sinners of the infernal doom that awaits them. The only source of redemption could be found beyond the wooden doors of the inner sanctum. He agonizingly pushed against them several times with all of his weakened strength. The heavy doors slowly opened. The large entrance was heavily laden with thickened cobwebs. He lit his oil lantern and picked up a broken stick to brush the stiff cobwebs away as he made a narrow path.

Ricardo's metal lantern illuminated a part of the unconfined vastness of the immense church. Wooden statues and

paintings belonging to times long past were decaying. Artwork from an age of darkness, witchcraft and heresy, showing the forces of good fighting against the forces of evil. Nothing had been moved or touched in that unforgettable capsule of antiquity. The many rows of empty pews gave Ricardo an unearthly feeling as he searched for the remote vestry. He felt as if someone was watching and following his movements. Suddenly there was a screeching, whining noise near him. A furry form swooped down towards him. It retreated when the bright light from his mirrored lantern shown in its horrid face. Ricardo lifted his glowing lantern. The high ceiling was full of clinging, cowering bats. The brightness made them flutter away to hide themselves in darkened corners. Their fluttering and fixed beady eyes filled Ricardo with unimaginable terror. But he kept repeating,

"I must find that diary, I must, I must!"

The apprehensive man reached the ruined vestry expecting misfortune at every turn. There were four walls. Which one could the coffer be in? Ricardo searched each bare wall carefully but found no trace of a clue. As he forebodingly sat down in despair, a curious design struck his attention. It was located an arms length from the stone floor and stood out with a hideous look. It was a frightful bas-relief carving of the angel of death. Ricardo crept slowly over to the bizarre image to study it in detail. The grim one foot figure was holding an hour glass in its potent hand as a symbol of the futility and brevity of a human life. The other hand held the grim reaper's metal scythe. A strange reflex made Ricardo touch the gruesome figure. As Ricardo's trembling hand stroked the deceptive sythe a sharp pain brought him to his senses. He was cut. Ricardo's touch moved the sharpened scythe making one end of the stone block open forward. He stayed wondering, even forgetting about his pain.

The aged coffer was there to the back of the secret opening! Ricardo pulled it out and walked over to a stone bench to remove its valued contents. He found a crumbling pearl rosary, Holy water, a silver crucifix and a diary. He hurriedly thumbed through the yellowed pages to look for the tragic story. The old priest had recorded everything that had happened during his long merciful ministry. Ricardo came to a small sketch of St. Michael trampling the unyielding Devil.

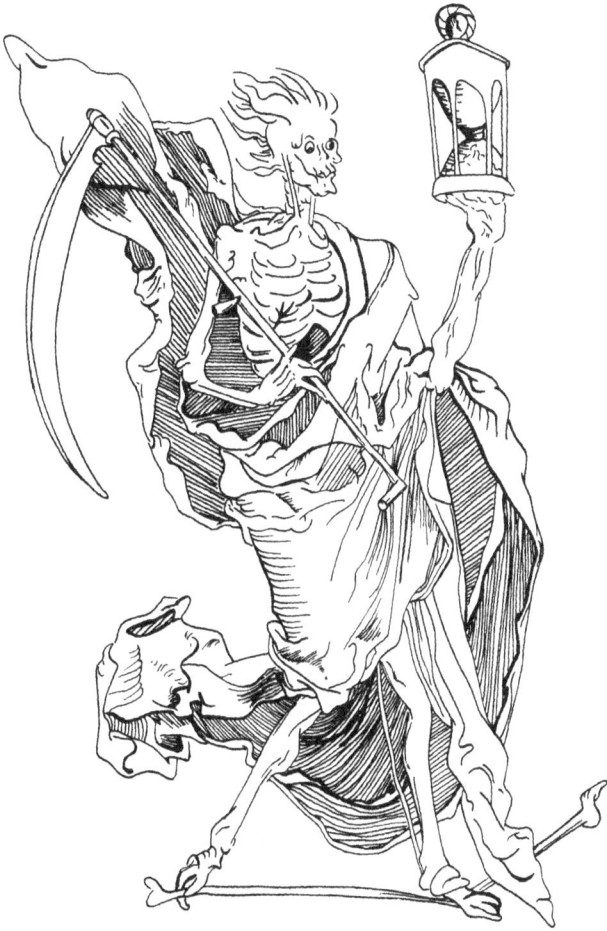

His weakened hands shook nervously as he continued to read the precious forgotten diary. The long departed priest had written,

"Late on a moonlit night, I was awakened by hard rapping at the rectory doors. Upon opening them I found an aged, humped woman asking for sanctuary from the bitter cold. She was dressed in black and her wide shawl covered all of her wrinkled face except for her peering, penetrating eyes."

"Father," she said. "I am close to death. I wish to have my confession heard and I want to tell you of a heavy burden that has plagued me for so many years."

"I invited her in, whereupon I heard her confession, and a most curious tale. The woman's story began in the year 1589 in the city of Mexico. The city was the central seat of the government of New Spain at the time. Most of the main section of the beautiful city was populated by the noble families of officials placed on assignment by the King of Spain. The viceroy, as the representative of the king, transplanted the finery and elegance of the European courts to the colonial city. The families of the soldiers lived modestly in the outskirts of the city. Although some of

them had seen bloody combat with mighty Cortez, they never arose above the stature of mere soldiers in the service of his majesty the king.''

Ricardo suddenly jumped up from the hard bench where he sat. He was certain he had felt a swift movement. As the small vestry was brightly lit he could see nothing in the tomblike room. His searching eyes glanced upon the angel of death and curiously the gory scythe was missing. He failed to investigate further, but rather sat back determinedly to continue reading. The exciting tale continued as it was related to the fray.

In September of that year, 1589, the king sent the count of Tarragona, Don Felipe Agustin de Mendoza, to the service of the viceroy, Luis de Velasco. The arrogant count and his daughter, Maria Dolores, arrived anxious to see the new lands that had become a part of the Spanish Empire. They saw that the capital city was teeming with activity as new buildings were being erected. The imposing cathedral rivaled those of the beloved mother country. The Count of Tarragona and his prudish daughter were given comfortable residence in a sumptuous home adjoining that of the viceroy, his wife, Doña Teresa, and their son, Juan de Velasco.

A week after the Mendozas had arrived, the viceroy and Doña Teresa held a grand ball in their honor at the magnificent palace. Luis de Velasco spared no expense with the lavish affair. To be certain the unwanted peasantry would be kept away from the royal palace on that special evening, Velasco posted an unpopular proclamation threatening them with imprisonment.

All of the snobbish aristocracy were in attendance although it was the coldest, blackest wintry night we had seen. The joyous laughter and revelry was so loud that it could be heard over great distances. It was on this very night that the self-assured son of the viceroy met Maria Dolores de Mendoza. She was a very proud and haughty young woman that was forever examining her physical appearance.

Velasco and Mendoza struck a warm friendship right from the beginning. They began to talk about their past achievements while Doña Teresa introduced Maria Dolores to her close friends. Their noble backgrounds and aspirations were quite similar. They were both from illustrious families and in their youth had attended the University of Salamanca, although at different times. Mendoza was nearly six years older. His frail wife had died when their daughter was very young. He had never remarried after his beloved wife's death and had dedicated his lonely life to his spoiled daughter. He admitted that maybe he had done too much for Maria through the solitary years but they were very close.

Velasco and Doña Teresa had married at a young age, but had been unable to have children. After several years Juan was born. The irritated viceroy confessed,

"My unscrupulous son is accustomed to having his way. I am very concerned by his carefree activities with the village girls. The flamboyant boy should seriously start considering matrimony. He needs a sensible, practical young woman such as your daughter to help him get settled. Besides, Juan is already twenty years old. Soon he will be past the proper marriageable age."

Feeling proud with de Velasco's complimentary remarks concerning his daughter, Mendoza added,

"I too feel my unattached daughter should marry soon. Maria Dolores is two years older than Juan."

Maria Dolores had two humble maids to attend to her slightest whims. Her uncontrolled selfishness often resulted in rabid mistreatment of the poor girls. Doña Teresa and Maria rejoined the count and viceroy.

After a gay and lively conversation that ended with Maria scolding her maids, the viceroy's wife was very complimentary of Maria Dolores. Doña Teresa told the elated count,

"Your outstanding daughter is an exceptionally fine young woman."

The quick-thinking viceroy sent one of the chamber servants to summon Juan to meet Señorita de Mendoza. Juan arrived shortly thereafter. He found himself being the steady listener to Maria Dolores' continuous talking. He was soon quite disturbed at being asked to be Maria Dolores' escort. The señorita's pride was made manifest by her having Juan promenade her around the immense ballroom.

The viceroy and count were rather pleased at how well their offspring seemed to be getting along. They soon saw a convenient marriage between their beloved children. The two plotting men retired to the palace library to discuss, then negotiate a marriage contract. The young couple would know of their mutual desire in good time. Right now it was best that Juan and Maria get to know each other better.

The ornate door to the library opened. Señora de Velasco quickly walked in. Putting her outstretched arms around both of theirs, she rapidly escorted them out of the room saying,

"The guests are asking for you. Your vital
company is needed at the ball."

Juan de Velasco and Señorita de Mendoza had danced several times that joyous evening. He had desired to dance with others, but his overbearing mother would hear nothing of it. The count and his coddled daughter returned home late that night. Juan knew nothing of what had transpired between his devious father and Count de Mendoza.

Juan retired to his room, upon arrival at the palace. His parents, however, felt in great need of a nightcap. Sipping at their drinks Doña Teresa said the first words,

"I found the dear girl very much to my
liking. She would make a lucky young man
such a wonderful wife."

She was then informed by her beaming husband about the entire conversation he had with Mendoza. The viceroy's wife wholeheartedly gave her approval to such a marriage agreement.

Doña Teresa and her future daughter-in-law met the following day to do some shopping at the market square. The elegant woman was filled with excitement.

"I was informed that a new cargo of gay
colored silks and fragrant perfumes have arrived. I honestly cannot contain my desire to
see them."

Teresa de Velasco gave Maria a mischievous smile. She would have to make plans for the forthcoming wedding. No date was set but it was never too soon to prepare for her new wardrobe.

Señora de Velasco and Maria Dolores were out bright and early at the crowded market place. Both cheerfully noticed the strong armed slaves unload the heavy trunks carrying the priceless merchandise. One merchant flatly stated,

"Doña Teresa de Velasco and her guest have first choice. It is they who can decide which trunks will be opened for their inspection."

It was a wonderful feeling to be treated with such attention and Maria Dolores relished every minute of it. It was a perfect day and they returned home pleasantly content with their valued prizes. The obedient servants tiredly walked behind carrying the purchases.

Juan, in the days that followed, kept himself busy with the sports of dueling with rapiers and horsemanship. His involved parents tried to encourage him to court Maria Dolores. He argued,

"The self-centered girl is much too concerned with herself and the all interesting topic of conversation is what she is going to do next."

His rebuffed parents insisted,

"It is to your benefit to marry someone in her social class."

His mother added,

"Someday you yourself might even be a distinguished count."

Juan failed to see the advantages saying,

"I could never marry one I believe could not make me happy. Above all, she is much older than I."

"But she is a very attractive young woman, Juan."

his mother added.

Laughingly he answered,

"My mother, the matchmaker."

Juan kissed her cheek and passed by his father quickly before they could continue the conversation saying,

"I will return after my morning ride."

Young Velasco often enjoyed riding out to the outskirts of the Aztec city. Upon reaching a rise above the city he would gaze out from the exact area where Cortez and his captains planned their assault on Tenochtitlan. The crisp morning air would fill Juan with joyous thoughts of the future. He also would envision the ideal woman of his dreams wherein they both would lead a storybook life of happiness. But this time, as he gazed from the rise he thought of his now confused future,

"There is no room in my plans for someone
like Maria Dolores. I could never love her!"
He countered.

Perhaps Juan wasn't quite giving Maria Dolores an opportunity to prove herself. Whatever the case, when he thought of her becoming a nagging, unattractive old woman he found the idea repugnant. He then rode off in a mad dash across the countryside.

Juan pressed his horse on as he bit his lip in disgust. Riding into the nearby Villa of San Geronimo his horse kicked the dry dust in a furious pace and frightened both chickens and townspeople along the way. He arrived at the local tavern and rushed in demanding a bottle of grape wine. He drank it within minutes, quickly asking for another. Being recognized as the son of the viceroy, he readily became the interesting topic of conversation. His unnatural behavior was very unbecoming for someone of his position. Be that as it may, Juan de Velasco continued his revelry until he was completely inebriated. He stumbled out of the small tavern in search of his horse.

"Trueno (Thunder)," he called out to his
horse as he laughingly taunted the village
folk. "Ah, my fine horse you are such a
faithful companion. Maybe you can take me
away from my problems and help me find the
'Dulcinea' of my dreams."

Juan awkwardly mounted his shying horse and rode off in search of the well to douse himself with the cool water. No one was at the community well as he dismounted, nearly falling. He poured a pail of water over his head. As the young man's vision returned, he could not tell whether or not he was dreaming. There was a young, beautiful girl several feet away from him, filling a fragile pitcher with water. Juan attempted to approach her, but she stepped away in fear. The elusive

47

girl had long silky hair that fell carressingly over her shoulders. She was rather poorly dressed, but her beauty would have made rags look like fine clothing. Juan's words stumbled out as he desperately tried to strike up a conversation.

"What is your name?"

He feebly asked. Young de Velasco was a sight to behold with his curly hair dripping wet as he desperately tried to steady himself. She began to walk away. He called and moved towards her. In his attempt to keep her from leaving he tripped and fell with a loud thud on the dry ground. He laughed at what a ridiculous spectacle he must have appeared to be to the bashful young woman. Juan again asked,

"Please don't leave! Who are you?"

She could not keep from smiling. Now, with the eyes of a coquette, she whispered softly, "Luisa Gertrudis de Panuelo." She dropped her fragrant kerchief as she stepped lightly away and disappeared as mysteriously as she had appeared.

Juan managed to raise himself as though he were in a state of ecstasy. He reached quickly for the perfumed cloth. The sweet fragrance of rose petals was the final touch to his overwhelming desire of seeing the alluring young maiden again. He rode home late that day, pulling the fine cloth out periodically to breathe in the dizzying aroma. Arriving at home he walked right past his inquisitive parents and went directly to his upstair's room. A servant was sent to summon Juan for the evening meal. He refused to eat saying his stomach was completely full.

"Another morsel would surely make it burst,"

the male servant repeated as he explained to Juan's waiting parents.

Luisa had left a deep impression upon Juan. Her soft melodious voice kept filtering through his active mind as he recalled her speaking to him. Yes, Juan's heart was captured by the young girl at the well. Maria Dolores would be no match.

Juan retired for the evening, but he was unable to keep his contemplating eyes closed much less sleep. His enraptured mind was thoroughly occupied with happy thoughts of Luisa.

He believed her to be the most beautiful girl in the world.

  "If she could only be mine," he said to
himself, "Then the old spinster Maria would
have to go off in search of another catch."

It was true Maria Dolores was far from being the ideal
woman. But for all practical purposes anyone would have
given his right arm to marry her. After all, Maria was
highly regarded at the European courts. She was King
Phillip's pride and joy. She also had her fair share of suitors.
If all this were true,

  "Then why had she not married long
before this?"

Maria Dolores had not found anyone to her liking. Juan de
Velasco was handsome, debonair, a man of the world,
educated and above all, the son of the viceroy.

  "He would be suitable," Maria thought.

Juan awoke early the following morning after a disturbed
sleep. The bright morning sun shone into his room in all of its
glory. It was a perfect day to do what he had already determined to do; see the enchanting Luisa.

A servant knocked loudly at his bedroom door as he dressed. Juan was about to answer when he decided to play a trick on Vicente saying,

"I'm still rather sleepy, I won't be getting up until later. Tell them I will join them for dinner. Will you please offer my respects to my parents?"

"Yes, but I will check in on you periodically to see if you are in need of anything," answered Vicente.

Juan placed his pillows and a few articles of clothing under the quilted covers to make it appear that he was still asleep. He felt this was much better than answering endless questions his domineering mother would ask at the breakfast table. After all, he had no desire to eat. Juan had to return to San Geronimo in search of the fair Luisa.

The young man's room was located on the second floor of the stately palace. But he was able to climb down on thick vines that grew along the side of the stone wall. Once down he carefully made his way to the stables where he saddled his graceful horse. He led Trueno out through a rear entry and soon found himself riding away as free as the breeze. Smiling along the way, Juan thought longingly of reaching San Geronimo. It was a five mile trip but to Juan it seemed more like fifty miles. As he arrived, he noticed the industrious villagers were already going about their daily business. Now Juan was confronted with a major problem. How could he find Luisa?

The viceroy's young son questioned a group of lively women that were taking their laundry to the broad lake for washing. He at first had difficulty trying to decide how to ask if they knew Señorita de Panuelo. Several giggled as Juan nervously stuttered when he found that an older matron would answer him. He was informed Luisa would be doing her morning shopping at the village market.

Juan bowed down at the waist as they moved on away from him. He could now breathe with a sigh of relief as he thought of his easy success. De Velasco rode on to the village market and found many there already bartering for agricultural products and livestock. The young man dismounted and tied his faithful steed to a post. He walked slowly about as his eyes searched for Luisa. After failing to find her, he returned to the market entry to be certain he would see all that might enter.

Juan had been waiting for awhile when he noticed a young girl walking with an older woman. His heart began to pound heavily as he thought it might be the one he had seen by the well. When they neared the market, the older woman walked away saying,"I will meet you at the church later." The young lady noticed Juan and smiled as she entered the market. He went after her immediately.

"Señorita, I would very much like to offer my sincere apology for my poor behavior yesterday. You see I had a pressing matter that troubled me deeply and I temporarily lost my head."

Feeling sorry for the young gentleman she answered,

"There is no need for an apology. What is it that is wrong?"

"Oh, nothing you should concern yourself with. It really isn't anything serious. Perhaps time will take care of it."

She then asked,

"Were you hurt by the fall yesterday?"

"Oh no," he laughingly answered, "just shaken up a little."

He introduced himself as Juan de Velasco and quickly asked,

"Was the woman you were with your mother?"

"Oh no," she answered,"she is my duenna." Feeling more at ease she added, "My mother died when I was a small child. My father hired a duenna to care for me ever since."

"I'm sorry to hear about your mother. How did she die?"

Luisa's eyes watered slightly as she began to recall her mother.

"We lived in Barcelona and were on our way to the New World. Many of the people on the ship were dying from a severe fever.

52

My poor mother was so worried I would become ill. But it was she who came down with the dreaded sickness. At times she would get better. I remember my exhausted father was greatly relieved one night when the fever had apparently broken. But she died by morning. Even after all these years, my lonely father has never gotten over her untimely death. He is a sergeant in the viceroy's guard and is constantly at work. I hardly ever see him. I sometimes think he prefers working all the time, instead of being at home. He has a great sense of guilt for my mother's death."

"What is your father's name?" Juan asked.

"He is Manuel Estevan de Panuelo," she answered proudly.

Juan presented himself to her as the son of the viceroy, stating,

"I will look into your father's duties. Maybe we can arrange for your father to have more free time to spend at home with you."

Luisa was initially taken aback by discovering she was speaking with the son of the viceroy. She promptly begged for his leniency at her being so open with one of his stature. He responded,

"Please don't think that way Luisa. I am a man like any other. I feel it is right for any young man and woman to converse regardless of position if they so wish."

Luisa was overjoyed. They both moved joyfully about as they walked from stall to stall checking the ripe fruits and vegetables. All of the bartering vendors appeared to know Luisa. She spoke to everyone in a friendly and familiar tone of voice. A few even failed to charge her for some of the things she had selected, saying,

"Luisa, your beauty and presence here is payment enough!"

She was well liked. It was quite a contrast between her and the sour Maria Dolores. Soon Luisa's basket was full and they both walked out of the active market.

"My duenna is at the church,"
Luisa stated as they walked through the wide exit.

"She is a very holy woman and makes it a
point to go pray to Saint Francis every day."

Juan offered to walk with her to the nearby church as he carried the filled basket for her. She shyly agreed and placed her gentle hand on his arm. The colorful birds chirped merrily and the playful children laughed contentedly in the ancient streets as Juan and Luisa slowly walked along. They soon arrived at the stately church and Luisa bid him farewell as she reached to open the ornate door. Juan wanted to follow her in.

"No you must not. I do not believe my
duenna would approve."

"At least promise I may see you again
soon,"
Juan pleaded.

"Perhaps there will be another time."

Juan charmingly kissed her hand and she disappeared behind the closed door. He returned to his spirited steed and briskly rode home.

Yes, Juan was a happy man. His surprised parents and the loyal servants noticed a marked improvement in his behavior. Doña Teresa, of course, gave all of the credit to Maria Dolores. After all, Maria had been spending more time at the palace trying to impress her son.

Juan's daily activities were interrupted by mental visions of the beautiful Luisa. Her captivating, bewitching beauty haunted his sleep at night and kept him from eating by day.

It seemed as though Juan could think of nothing else but her. He found himself with an uncontrollable desire to see the fascinating Luisa. He had a happy thought. She had informed him she made daily journeys to the artesian well for water. Perhaps he could wait for her and feel her refreshing presence once again. Returning to the village well, Juan found the area deserted. He patiently waited for Luisa to appear. He would turn quickly in anxious hope when a sudden noise or movement would catch his attention. The minutes painfully turned into hours and yet she did not come. Many pretty girls had passed by, but none were quite like his enticing Luisa.

The previously calm weather began to change drastically as Juan waited for her. The clear sky grew dark with thick nebulous clouds. The loud thunder and flashing lightning drew steadily nearer. The melancholy wind seemed to call Luisa's enchanting name! L-O-O-E-E-E-S-A-A-A. L-O-O-E-E-E-S-A-A-A. Her ever present vision made him hear dismal voices in the gloomy wind. Juan finally gave up and decided to leave. He moved on to his frightened horse and lifted his foot to place it in the leather stirrup. He was thoroughly disappointed. It began to rain heavily as he mounted his horse to leave.

Nearing the palace Juan noticed a detachment of soldiers standing guard at the massive doors.

"There was an attempt on your father's life,"

Juan was told as he identified himself and was allowed to enter. He caught his excited mother's attention while she was in the midst of a conversation. Moving quickly towards him, she became very emotional as she described in detail how a bloodthirsty assassin nearly killed his father.

Hearing a great deal of commotion in the social hall, Juan heard his father exclaiming to the inquisitive gathering,

"This is the fiber of the Spanish soldier. Manuel Estevan de Panuelo epitomizes the true spirit of valor."

Puzzled, Juan questioned his father,

"What did de Panuelo do?"

De Velasco promptly answered,

"He courageously gave his life for mine. A traitorous assassin was captured and his contemptible head was speedily hacked off with a broadax on the executioner's block."

Viceroy de Velasco resumed explaining the interesting particulars to his prying listeners as his son stood in complete silence. Juan, overcome with shock, left to his room. He lay on his bed thinking of her.

"Poor Luisa, what she must be going through right now. I wish I could do something for her. She must feel terribly sorrowful. The poor girl is left without a family, helpless and alone."

The following morning, Juan found his family and guests gathered at the breakfast table. Count Mendoza and Maria were engaged in amusing conversation. All were in good spirits and it appeared as though the frightening events of the previous day had been all but too soon forgotten. Sitting down to eat Juan brought it to light again, by asking,

"Was anything done for the guard's family, father?"

Taken by surprise, Doña Teresa immediately answered for her husband,

"Why of course son, your father will graciously provide for the care of his esteemed guard's family."

As she expected, this was very well received by the palace guests. Although Juan knew it was for appearance sake, he pressed the issue on.

"Would it be appropriate if I make the presentation to the bereaved family as your personal representative, father?"

Believing that it would meet with his wife's approval, de Velasco answered affirmatively. Doña Teresa interjected into the conversation,

"Juan has always been such a considerate young man."

Turning to Maria she added,

"Juan would make any young woman a wonderful husband."

Ignoring his mother's last statement, Juan excused himself and left.

Soon after young de Velasco found out where Luisa's modest home was located. He decided to go to her home and offer his condolences. Arriving there he knocked at the wooden door. Juan impatiently waited for her to answer. Expecting to see Luisa when the door opened, he was met face to face with the bewildered duenna. He presented himself as the viceroy's son, Juan de Velasco, saying,

"I am here representing my father to express sincere sympathies to the next of kin. I understand he has a daughter."

"Why yes," the duenna answered, "please come in. She will be most happy to see you. I

am quite glad the viceroy has taken such an
interest in those that serve him.''

The duenna led him to the room where the family altar was
located. He found her kneeling, praying silently. The ig-
norant duenna introduced him. Not making known that he
knew her Juan said,

"Siento mucho su pesar (I'm very sorry
about your burden).''

Luisa came to tears and the unaware woman thought
nothing about his embarassing her. He quickly added,

"You will be cared for through a generous
pension provided by the viceroy.''

The young woman with a trembling voice asked him to
thank Viceroy de Velasco for his kindness. Turning to the
duenna, he asked her,

"Would it be appropriate for me to check
in to make sure things are well?''

"Of course, we would welcome the son of
the viceroy to our humble home whenever it
pleases him.''

Juan began to visit Luisa at her home from then on. Arriving with a gift, he would offer a bouquet of flowers to both
her and her duenna.

"They are beautiful,'' both would respond.

"You must not trouble yourself by wasting
so much of your valuable time with us,'' the
duenna stated.

"It is no trouble at all. I feel it is my duty.
Luisa's father saved my father's life!''

One fine Sunday, the Velasco family went to mass as usual at the magnificent cathedral. The count and his daughter accompanied them. Maria Dolores had tried without success to catch Juan's attention. She had been notified by her father of her impending marriage to Juan. Maria was overjoyed and felt he would make a very proper husband.

The viceroy's grand coach arrived at the cathedral. The swift coachman rushed to open the door. All turned to see the noble families as they entered the church to be seated. Juan noticed a girl dressed in white silk and lace mantilla (veil). He felt it could be no other than Luisa. She turned, smiled and their love filled eyes met. He noticed that her duenna saw them. She glared a sly disapproval. The elderly woman was well aware they were experiencing something more than a casual relationship.

Luisa's serene beauty seemed almost unreal. Juan felt she should belong only to him. The following Monday when he arrived at Luisa's home, she was alone. She had asked her duenna to do the shopping without her in anticipation of his arrival. De Velasco suggested they could go on a leisurely stroll. Luisa agreed saying,

"My duenna will be gone for another hour or so. You must promise to bring me home before that,"

"Certainly I will," Juan assured her. "We will go down by the lake, spend a short time there and return within an hour."

They held hands as they walked pleasantly along involved in a lovers' intrigue. Juan pulled her to the side of a tall building where he passionately kissed her exquisite neck and then on her tender lips. With throbbing hearts they left to continue the walk after hearing suspicious voices nearby. He took her to a hidden place where they could be alone. Juan told Luisa of his deep love for her. The savage passions he had for Luisa erupted. He took her into his longing arms and eagerly kissed her. The mutual desire soon became inflamed with the need of fulfillment. Their vibrant bodies pressed ever closer as they surrendered uncontrollably in compliance with the act of love. It was not a mere enjoyment of a sexual fantasy but a spiritual bond that made their precious love for one another more complete.

Inspite of the protective duenna's objections, Juan and Luisa spent more time together. Soon the townspeople began to gossip about their strange tempestuous love affair. It was brought to the attention of the viceroy. De Velasco questioned his disconcerted son about the disturbing rumors. Juan admitted they were true and frankly added he was deeply in love with her.

His righteous father was in a state of outrage.

"How dare you say you are in love with a coarse peasant. Do you not realize this would cause shame and scandal to our noble name? You must cease your reckless venturing and think seriously abour marrying Maria Dolores. The distinguished count and I have already discussed a marriage agreement between you and Maria and she has already been told!"

"How could you make such an arbitrary agreement without first consulting me. I will not marry her!"

Juan replied angrily.

With this the offended viceroy left the room. Luis de Velasco stormed into his wife's bedchamber to share the distasteful news of their impetuous son. The viceroy's wife was at first shocked but then cunningly reassured her rash husband.

"Surely, Juan will soon tire of the peasant. He will agree with us and see the advantages of marrying Maria Dolores de Mendoza. This village tramp has virtually nothing to offer and besides our intelligent son is a practical young man."

The soothing conversation with his cautious wife soon made him forget his anger. They both settled down to develop a concerted plan. Maria Dolores was later consulted. She agreed with their idea of impressing upon Juan the recklessness of his actions. She was convinced that with time her own persuasion and desireability would be the victor and Luisa the loser. Doña Teresa de Velasco knew how to play the game well. She instilled within Maria Dolores the determination to succeed and never place herself in a position of defeat.

60

To assure the accomplishment of their desire it was proposed to occupy Juan's time with more social events and entertainment which would involve the pair. The firm scheme was doomed to failure. Juan spent less time at home and sought every opportunity to break away.

In time Luisa was heavy with child and Juan sought his parent's consent to marry her. They bitterly refused and opposed any marriage with a peasant girl. Juan's father wanted the substantial wealth of both the Mendoza and Velasco families to be combined. As a spiteful act meant to punish both Juan and Luisa, the pernicious viceroy put a stop to the vital pension. With this he expected his dependent son to succumb to the pressure of his significant threats.

Luisa was sad and weeped when Juan gave her the somber news of the refusal. He told Señorita de Panuelo that his love for her would never die and vowed to continue in his struggle to marry her. Not letting his parents know, Juan continued to support Luisa and her duenna.

Luisa de Panuelo gave birth to an adorable child. Juan cherished the tiny infant. It seemed as though the two were brought even closer together. They were ecstatically happy although they were not allowed to marry.

As the joyful year passed, Luisa gave birth to another child. Now Juan was certain his obdurate parents would no longer deny a marriage between them. He would confront them with the question of giving legitimate birth to his offspring. Luisa herself was maltreated by the village folk and had to remain mostly indoors. The duenna was compassionate and cared for Luisa and the two little ones.

Maria Dolores was outraged when she was notified Luisa had two children fathered by Juan de Velasco. Having always had her way, Señorita de Mendoza pressed the commitment to their marriage contract. She soon faced the viceroy and his wife with a strenuous objection saying,

> "I have been waiting for my marriage to Juan for over four years. I can no longer wait! You either comply with the marriage agreement or my father shall inform the king about the entire matter. You will be recalled back to Spain in disgrace!"

They were both left grief stricken. Juan was immediately confronted when he returned to the depressing palace. The volatile issue was brought to the surface and Doña Teresa did all in her power to degrade Luisa. Was Luisa to assume all of the blame? She was talked of as a sinful harlot with no other desire than to fulfill her sexual appetite with a helpless victim. She seduced their defenseless son and therefore, Juan should feel no love for her. They issued an ultimatum,

"Either you marry Maria Dolores de Mendoza or you will find yourself disowned. You will no longer be regarded as our son!"

Juan was speechless.

"How can I support Luisa and our children?"

he thought to himself. The young man was filled with sorrow. Hereditary wealth was all he knew. Physical labor was reserved for only those of common heritage.

"I must have some time to think about this,"

he said. The viceroy sharply retorted,

"We can no longer overlook the scandal the affair is causing against the family name! Not even our noble stature can withstand the stain of corruption. The social classes are well defined. Sheer mixture as you well know is an act punishable by the seriousness of the crime. Were you anyone else but my son, you would have been cast off and shamed publicly. If you do not make a correct and immediate determination, I will be forced to make you a homeless, neglected wanderer."

Luisa could scarcely believe what she heard Juan say when he returned. He did not respond to her gentle kiss when she lovingly embraced him. His troubled eyes would not meet hers as she asked,

"Are you really considering doing what your parents have demanded?"

He did not answer. Since Juan now appeared to reject her, Luisa began to sob loudly. Juan quickly added,

"I do not know how I would be able to support you or our children."

Luisa pleaded,

"I'm sure we can make it somehow. If you really love us, I know we can work it out!"

"You know that I love you and the children,"

he replied. Placing his arms around Luisa, he calmed her with his words.

"I will try to reason with my parents. If we discuss things clearly then we might reach a mutual solution."

Juan returned to his home the following morning. His parents were angry and upset when he entered.

"Where have you been all night? I suppose you spent the night in the bed of that village strumpet again!"

His mother screamed. He was soon whimpering and confused with the unceasing onslaught projected by his heartless parents. The viceroy even thought of banishing Luisa and the children from New Spain.

"Oh no," Juan begged, "I could not bear to lose my children!"

Viceroy de Velasco answered,

"It is possible for you and Maria Dolores to raise the guiltless children. After all they are yours. Are they not? This way you can give them your name legitimately and they will be true Velascos. Don't you agree Teresa?"

"Oh yes, I am sure the count and Maria would agree. Although Luisa is not of royal blood, this is offset by your noble lineage, Juan. You yourself know that I am a cousin of the Duke of Leon. Your ancestors have sat alongside the throne of the kings of Spain."

"Yes, I know only too well my dear mother."

She added,

"The children are still very young and would never have to know who their real mother is. The lowly peasant wench must consider the well being of your offspring. Your bastardly children will be well educated and raised in wealth and finery as Maria Dolores' very own. She has given her humane consent to this. Perhaps one could become a viceroy himself one day. Luisa would be well cared for and kept at the convent."

They felt it would be a very fair arrangement. Juan was at a loss for words. Thinking he had no choice in the matter and that he was being realistic, he decided in favor of his parents wishes.

"Surely," Juan thought, "Luisa will be capable of understanding the merits of the decision. After all, I will still be able to see her regularly and we must, above all else, consider the children's welfare."

With the false belief that he was not being selfish, Juan went on to relate the news to a depressed Luisa. Falling to her knees she desperately pleaded with Juan.

"Please, I beg of you, please change your mind. How can you in one instant throw away the love and happiness we have experienced together? I could not go on living if you took our children away from me. Please, Juan..."

Juan stopped her from continuing by saying,

"You will still be nearby and well cared for at the convent. I will go to see you every day.

65

Our children will have everything and enjoy a
rich life rather than exist in poverty."
She yelled out,

"No Juan, you can not do this to me! Am I
to be a prisoner at the convent for the rest of
my life and never see my children again. What
is my crime except that I love you."

Luisa held on to him. As he moved in an attempt to free
himself from her, he dragged her on the floor. The poor girl
soon became hysterical and threw objects about the room
with a crashing, thundering sound. Once again she hopelessly
held on to Juan but he tore himself away from her desperate,
pleading and clutching body.

The duenna ran terrified into the room after hearing the
earth shattering struggle. She sought to protect Luisa after
learning of the situation by scolding Juan.

"How could you agree with your unfeeling,
uncaring parents? Please forgive me for
speaking thusly to the son of the viceroy, but I
believe I am right with what I am saying!"

After calming down a little, she added,

"You cannot take away her children. She
has no mother. Her father died for your
father's life. You robbed her of her pride. She
has nothing left but her children. Juan, you
must seriously reconsider your position."

Luisa continued to cry without consolation in her duenna's
arms. Juan, rather than listening to the wise elderly woman,
stormed out of the house angrily shouting,

"I will return for the children tomorrow!
Have their clothing ready!"

As Juan rode furiously home, new thoughts entered his
troubled and confused mind. He had a bothersome idea.

"Could the meddlesome duenna arouse
some of the local villagers to her and Luisa's
aide and keep me from getting my children?
Would they dare to hide them from me?"

These and other nagging beliefs flashed through his swim-
ming head until he decided to return on that very afternoon
rather than on the following day.

66

The worried duenna tried desperately to get Luisa to control herself. She, however, was totally hysterical and the poor duenna was forced to slap her violently in an attempt to snap her out of it. The forlorn girl was a pathetic sight, finally fainting limply to the floor. Not knowing exactly what to do, the duenna thought of going to the curandera for help. The innocent children were alseep in the room so she felt certain they would be safe until her quick return.

Arriving at the curandera's home the alarmed duenna was informed by her neighbors she was near the lake's edge seeking medicinal herbs. Suddenly the seconds dragged into everlasting minutes as she raced till near exhaustion toward the broad lake. As her agitated heart beat heavily, she knew that she could not stay away too long.

> "The children might awaken," she
> thought. "Luisa may be hurt!"

Images of Luisa's fainting forced her to run even faster; close to the point of stumbling.

Juan hurried into the sanctuary of the palace. The duenna's words kept going through his crowded mind. He pictured Luisa's pleading, tortured face. Were his parents wrong?

Juan screamed out, "What should I do?"

Startled by Juan's screaming, Doña Teresa and the viceroy rushed out of the library. They had been discussing Juan's and Maria's marriage. What a grand ceremony it would be. Juan sobbingly related,

> "I explained to Luisa what we had dis-
> cussed concerning the best interests of our
> children. She wouldn't listen. In fact, I was
> blamed for actually seducing the girl. Now I
> am not sure of what is right. Did I really take
> advantage of Luisa? Did I use her sorrow over
> her father's death to suit my own purposes?"

Doña Teresa readily took advantage of the situation. She quickly replied,

> "My dear, dear son. How unselfish you
> are. Can't you see she is using you. She knows
> she has lost. What else can she do now, but
> make you feel guilty for what she is guilty of.

Her duenna cannot do anything else but defend Luisa. After all, what will she do after Luisa goes to the convent and you have your children. There will no longer be any need for her services."

Juan began to calm down. Doña Teresa held on to him, comforting him. His father added,

"Juan you must listen to your mother. You know your mother is very wise and is always right when it comes to the character of people. I have always come to her for such advice. She has never failed me."

Juan quickly moved away and said,

"I must go for my children now. I cannot wait until tomorrow. You are right. The duenna is a very convincing woman. She will turn the townspeople against me. I must go."

Doña Teresa yelled out to Juan,

"Wait, Juan you will need some help."

She turned to the viceroy, and said,

"You must send some of your soldiers along with Juan. There is bound to be trouble."

Juan and several soldiers of the viceroy's guard arrived at Luisa's home on the afternoon of that fateful day of October 1st, 1593. He went prepared to take the children. Luisa was to be taken to the convent of the Immaculate Conception. As they neared the commodious hut they heard unearthly screams and deafening wailing. Juan and the war seasoned soldiers rushed to the building without reigning their horses. They frantically sought to reach the heavy wooden door. It was locked. Juan heard a child's unforgettable scream. It rang through his ears as he ordered,

"Break the door open, we must get in there!"

Two of the strongest pushed against it and the door buckled with their combined strength. It crashed onto the floor, tearing pieces of adobe as the hinges ripped away from the supports. Luisa stood there with demented eyes staring into another world. She held a naked keen edged dagger, turned, ready to strike herself. Grabbing her stiffened arm before she could plunge it deep into her yearning heart, Juan shockingly asked,

"Why are you trying to do this? Why do
you want to kill yourself?"

Blood already dripped from the thirsty dagger. Juan instinctively knew and shook her senseless body violently.

"Oh my God, what have you done?"

Pushing her aside with a savage thrust he found the two children in a pool of crimson blood. A scarlet stained note was pinned onto a soiled blanket that covered their lifeless unknowing bodies. Why did they have to suffer such a horrible death at the hands of the mother who gave them life? Why were they the naive victims of an overpowering lust for material possessions?

Their terror stricken father read with tears streaming down from his disbelieving eyes,

"Beloved Juan, I cannot bear the thought
of living without you, or losing our dear
children. Now it seems that I have nothing to
live for. If I cannot have my sweet children
with me in life, then I will take them with me
in death. May God forgive me for what I am
about to do!"

Juan felt bitterness and anger at experiencing such a terrifying nightmare. His immediate reaction was one of contempt and hatred for the helpless Luisa.

"If I had only listened to my mother
sooner. She was right."

Turning to Luisa he yelled,

"If I had only known. Luisa you cared for
no one but yourself!"

Luisa had apparently lost all reason. She failed to recognize Juan nor had any conception at all of what was taking place. His anger only increased as he yelled,

"Take her!"

The poor girl was treated unmercifully by the heartless angry soldiers. She tripped and struck her head on a jagged rock which opened a deep gash on her once flawless forehead. Blood ran streaking down her beaten face but she

felt nothing. They bound her gory wrists tightly with a lariat and half pulled her, half dragged her to the dark rat infested dungeon. She was pushed into a murky cell where she lay on the scattered straw as the revolting rats sought to nibble at her motionless ankles.

The sergeant-at-arms went on to inform Viceroy de Velasco,

> "Your excellency, I beg my intrusion but I
> have urgent news for you."

> "Come, come my man, give it to me and be
> off with you. I have very important business
> to attend to."

He went on to relate the sorrowful news concerning the brutal slaying of the angelic children.

> "We arrived at Luisa de Panuelo's home
> for the children. After entering we found
> them wrapped with a crimson cloth, made red
> by their own flowing blood."

The viceroy's eyes opened wider as he heard the gruesome details of the vicious murders. Without hesitating a moment, he went on to tell the ghastly story to his wife.

Without batting an eye, Doña Teresa readily saw the advantages of the situation.

> "We must count our blessings my dear hus-
> band. With the offspring out of the way,
> killed by their own mother, we have to offer
> no explanations to anyone as to their
> presence. Maria Dolores nevertheless was
> reluctant in taking them as her own. It was
> only on her father's request that she agreed.
> No one will ever know the true story of the en-
> tire distasteful affair. We must, however,
> make an example of Luisa for the distress she
> has put our son through and especially the
> pain she has caused us. There were many times
> I thought of how she would be the death of
> me. We must demonstrate to the public that
> such immoral behavior cannot be condoned.
> There must never be another incident as this
> one. They must never again consider

themselves as worthy of uniting with the nobility. We must make her suffer. Of course, she must also pay for the death of the children.''

The viceroy agreed. The public sentiment would have to be on their side. No one would condone such an act from anyone.

Still in shock, Juan left Luisa's home to summon the priest of the San Geronimo mission. The benevolent priest delivered the last rites for the children as curious onlookers gathered outside the depressive home. The village carpenter was notified and he took two small wooden boxes to be used as plain coffins for the slain infants. Juan could no longer remain there. He desperately needed to be with his family. He tried pushing his way through the large group of people already assembled at Luisa's home. The grim news spread from mouth to ear as excitement electrified the bewildered listeners. A soldier noticed Juan was having trouble in getting through the growing crowd and quickly pushed the struggling people out of his way. Finally away from the boisterous crowd, the soldier walked ahead of Juan as he led him to his horse.

The duenna had already heard of the grisly murders. She desperately tried to get information from the people as to Luisa's whereabouts. No one would answer her. She was only pushed away. Weak from exhaustion, she fell to the ground. As she raised herself, she caught a glimpse of Juan getting ready to leave. The old woman rushed to reach him before his leaving. Getting in Juan's way, she once again fell to her injured knees. The alert soldier ran to his aide.

"Where is Luisa? Please tell me, Juan, I beg of you. Is she all right?''

As Juan turned to look into her imploring face, he said,

"She will be punished for what she has done. She will die, but not by her own hand!''

The elderly woman raised herself from the ground. She began to cry hysterically. The soldier yelled from a distance,

"Get out of the way old woman!''

Juan began to ride away. The duenna could no longer control the hurt she felt for Luisa and her two children. She yelled to Juan,

"You are the murderer. You and your
ruthless parents are the real murderers!"
Just then the guard reached the duenna and hit her as he
asked,
"What do you know about the murders?"
Juan had stopped his horse. He turned to see her. She had
once again fallen to the hardened ground. The desolate
woman lay there terrified and helplessly cried. Juan de
Velasco could not reply. He only stared. The soldier turned to
him,
"I will take her to the viceroy. She will be
punished for her insolence."
He pulled the duenna away. What had taken place, had
luckily gone unnoticed by the crowd. The mobbish crowd
was spellbound by a captivating speaker. A statesman? Yes,
one endowed with the gift of speech. An orator who could
sway anyone into following the course he desired.
"How can anyone commit such an ungodly
act of vengeance against the flesh of her
flesh?" he asked. "Is it the deed of a mad
woman or an evil witch?"
"A witch!" they all shouted. "Only a witch
could derive pleasure from the killing of little
ones to satisfy her lust for blood."
Meanwhile the duenna arrived at the palace. She was immediately taken to the viceroy. He angrily questioned the
scared woman.
"What did you say to my son?"
The duenna was ready to collapse. She could not answer.
Luis de Velasco yelled as he raised himself from his chair.
"Where were you when she murdered her
children?"
The duenna cried out,
"I know nothing of the murders, sire. I was
gone and knew nothing of what had taken
place until I was notified by one of the vil-
lagers."
He tossed a bag of gold coins at her feet.
"Take this money and leave the city. If you
dare to return, you will be arrested as an ac-

74

complice to the murders, and most probably
be executed in the same manner as Luisa will
be. You will be tortured, then burned!''

She was promptly escorted out of the capital city. The pitiful woman thought to herself,

"There is nothing I can do. I would gladly
give my life if Luisa would be spared. But she
would still be severely punished. And what
could I say? There is no way I could help her.
My knowledge of the circumstances before
the murders, could only hurt her. The viceroy
would surely treat Luisa even more harshly.
His excellency would be certain to contradict
my story. The people would never believe me.
If only I had not left her.''

She stood there alone and helpless. She began to cry again,

"God, please help her!''

A funeral mass was held for the slain children at the San Geronimo mission. The church bells rang out their doleful tones as the sorrow filled people converged at the main entrance. There was much to talk about.

"Did you hear?'' They would ask curious
visitors from nearby towns. "A horrible crime
was committed near our very doorsteps!''

The story became increasingly more sensationalized as it spread through greedy listeners. This was the most exciting event for decades in the area and soon everyone was caught within the grasp of the theatrical side show atmosphere. Imbecile and sane alike were overcome with such a scandalized fervor that even the most saintly would have surely suffered from their vindictive hands.

All settled in to listen as the inspired priest delivered his welcome sermon.

"She is the devil's tool and will burn in the
fires of hell for all eternity for the senseless
murders of those innocent children!''

The emotional crowd became thought filled with the extreme desire to seek retribution. Pointing to the dead bodies he added,

"The unfortunate children have arisen and

are now in the heavenly presence of the Lord.
There is no need for anyone to worry about
their saintly souls now!''

The black painted coffins were thereafter lowered into a deep sepulcher that was dug for them on the church floor near the main altar. As the stirred priest delivered the final eulogy he shouted to the spellbound mourners,

"The godless woman must be punished!''

The throng at the church was on the verge of passionate violence. The rapid events that were taking place would set the dramatic stage for her popular trial.

A heretofore unfelt excitement filled the thick air. All discussed the inevitable verdict beforehand and were positive only one conclusion would be reached. To add to the local gossip, some speculated Luisa had a pact with the Devil.

"He appears to her in the form of a dog.
She suckles the devil dog from a certain breast
where it puts its head to draw her succulent
blood. The devil repays her nourishment by
granting her demoniac powers. No one is safe
as long as she is around.''

Suddenly a shock among the populace grew increasingly morbid by the minute. The San Geronimo priest flung the church doors wide open and screamed for help. He had found the fresh graves of the infants reopened and the coffins lay tossed about empty. A timely addition to the case? Who was responsible? No one knew, but Luisa most certainly had something to do with it or did she? This caused an outrage amongst the already horrified people.

"Luisa is evil,'' they all would say.

The local Inquisitors were immediately notified concerning the case of a suspected witch. They, in turn, pointed out that the matter had to be presented to the Suprema, the policy-making council within the Spanish Inquisition in Spain. The civil authorities, however, sought every means to persuade the judges to issue a local directive. The confused judges were divided in their opinions and wished for more evidence that Luisa was indeed a witch. They finally bowed to public sentiment and the viceroy's pressure. On October 10, 1593 an auto-da-fe, a public declaration of the Inquisition's ruling, was held in the City of Mexico.

No condemned woman could have suffered more. The tribunal of the Inquisition sat in her judgement. They were dressed in black and wore conical hoods.

> "Why did you commit such a diabolical
> deed?"

each would ask.

Luisa stood stupified and failed to answer to flagrant charges brought against her. One spoke in her defense by stating she had been deceived and tricked by the Devil into wickedness. But it was now believed she was a heretic.

> "She had cast a spell upon the helpless son
> of the viceroy through her magnetic beauty."

They mumbled in the audience.

Juan, seated next to his parents, listened attentively as a case of witchcraft and heresy was built up against the doomed Luisa. He began to feel remorse and guilt. The duenna's words kept nagging at him,

> "You are the murderer. You and your
> ruthless parents are the real murderers!"

Juan could hear the burdensome words over and over again in his mind. He recollected vexatious events which had taken place before the murders.

The inquisition continued. Luisa would be put to the test to determine beyond doubt she was indeed a witch. She was stripped naked in the crowded courtroom. Her thinned arms were tied at the wrists. She was pulled up with a curious contraption so that her nude body was raised and suspended inches above the stone floor.

> "Search for the devil's mark!"

the inquisitor general ordered.

Juan's guilt increased as he watched Luisa's legs and arms stretched and her body shaved to facilitate the examination. Recalling to mind the cherished moments of the love and happiness they had experienced together made him emotional. He grew steadily nauseous as he watched Luisa's body ravaged by heartless seducers. Was it jealousy or hatred he felt? Whatever the case, it was clear to see Juan could not stand much more of it. The search for the brand new witches were supposed to be given upon initiation continued. Upon finding a birthmark, the witch hunters shouted to the impatient onlookers.

"The devil's mark is here!"

Among those who sat discussing the outcome of the exciting trial were the viceroy, his wife, the count and Maria Dolores. Doña Teresa would at times glance at her troubled son to see how he was reacting to the situation. She fostered an uneasy feeling that he would break down and lose control. A woman's intuition? Perhaps, but she would have to discuss it with her husband. Before this they had deemed it prudent for Juan to attend.

> "The observant people can see for them-
> selves, Juan shares no guilt in the murders.
> He was only one of her victims!"

They agreed it was for the best. The tension now mounted within her as she observed her son clenching his fists and gritting his teeth.

Maria Dolores sat bewildered, studying the whole affair. She was possibly a victim of circumstances. The prime of her life was rapidly passing before her eyes. She may have been too picky in the past in her selection of a mate. She, however, had determined to marry now despite the obstacles. "Juan's involvement with Luisa can be overlooked," she thought. She believed he would get rid of his foolhardiness prior to marriage and could be a better husband. His fathering the children made her quite angry. But she most certainly did not want to be the woman scorned.

Maria's thoughts were interrupted when an immediate order was passed to do the final test so that the accused's guilt could be proven for all to see. A sharp instrument called a pricker would be used to stick into the birthmark. If it caused her no pain or bleeding, then she was without doubt guilty of witchcraft.

The witch-hunters were conducting their investigation with appalling ferocity. With added prodding from the Inquisition they contemplated using fiendish devices of torture to extract a confession. The pricking would be a gruesome preliminary to satisfy the wanton appetites of the participants. Juan stood horror struck at learning of the intent of the court. Racing to stop the pricking he threw himself at Luisa's feet crying for forgiveness. Caught by surprise but quickly reacting to the situation, the viceroy had him ushered out of the courtroom. Resisting, Juan shouted,

"She is not guilty, we are!"

There was a mass of confusion with the new change in the tide of events. Doña Teresa saw fit to leave temporarily. She graciously excused herself. Maria Dolores wanted to leave also but her wise father believed it would be far too conspicuous. Convinced that ugly gossip would follow Juan's disgraceful behavior, Maria Dolores could not comprehend why Juan should react thusly towards a peasant and disregard her.

The viceroy returned and explained,

"Our sensitive son has been overcome by
the dreadful experience of witnessing such a
trial. He is undoubtedly still under the witch's
influence. He can no longer reason logically.
We beg forgiveness for the shameful interruption."

Luisa was still in a state of shock. Juan's reaction had apparently gone unnoticed by her. Man-handled and tortured, her once senstive flesh felt no pain.

"The final proof, obviously their is no
question her terrible master is the Devil!"
the witch-finders announced.

Luisa was put through even more torture in an attempt to get a confession. But she would not speak, or could not speak. Through the most cruel of tortures there were sometimes cries of anguish, but she did not speak.

Onlookers caught in the consuming fever of the trial offered themselves as witnesses against the accused. One admitted seeing Luisa change shape which was a power only the Devil could have given her. Another swore she had raised storms on the lake of Tenochtitlan and ruined the crops with magic poisons. Several confirmed Luisa weekly attended the aquelarre, the "field of the he-goat," in the frontier town where she lived. The site reportedly lay near where the river known as the stream of Hell ran. There Satan's throne was said to stand and Luisa presented the souls of her dead children in exchange for immortality. Finally, Luisa Gertrudis de Panuelo was pronounced a murderess and a witch and sentenced to death by fire.

Juan was temporarily locked into an adjoining room.

Pounding his fist against the wall, it was plainly visible he was guilt ridden in his betrayal of Luisa. He resented his parents. He had lost his family. Now his conscience would plague his sanity. After the termination of the trial Juan was confined to his bedchamber. The viceroy's physician declared the young man had an ailment which required immediate attention. Arriving with leeches, his associates unhesitatingly began the process of bleeding the patient.

Doña Teresa and the viceroy knew very well what troubled Juan. But they genuinly believed he should be thankful they had brought out Luisa's true nature. The physician would be left to do what was necessary. After this, the people would have to believe Juan's behavior was caused by her witchery. Doña Teresa would reason with Maria Dolores. It would cause her no embarrassment now that Luisa was formally declared a witch.

The whole affair of the trial created much excitement in the colonial city. The execution was to take place on the evening of that dark overcast Friday, October 13, 1593. People from everywhere gathered in the public square to see Luisa's death. As the hour of her demise drew near, one could hear the clacking of the large wheels of the wooden cart on the cobblestones. It moved agonizingly slow. Luisa's face could be seen from between the evenly spaced openings of the Death Cart. No one shall ever forget those terrifying eyes. They were opened wide. They looked like the frightened eyes of a fox as the hunter's dogs draw near for the kill. Her once beautiful hair had turned gray and her gracious face aged with sorrow.

She was laughed at and jeered at as the heavy cart passed by.

"Burn her, burn her at the stake!"
they cried. Some picked up nearby stones and cast them upon her. When the executioner's cart finally reached its destination, Luisa was pulled out by a coarse rope that was tied to her bleeding wrists. Poor Luisa's bare feet stumbled on the sharp, jagged stones and she fell to the merciless ground. She was then dragged up to the fire ready post by the hooded executioner. Members of the Inquisition encircled her as she was tied with a metal chain to the stake without a struggle.

They raised long crosses and chanted incantations to cast the evil spirits from her infected body and soul.

The treacherous fire was lit with the torches and, as Luisa burned, she began calling for her dead children.

"Come to me, please come to me!"
All could hear her say.

Luisa's tortured body twisting horribly in the blazing fire stood dominant against the vast sky which was already filled with darkness. Her closing spirit frightened everyone as she wailed loudly. She continued to cry pleadingly,

"Please don't take my children away from me!"

The devouring fire ate up the poor girl's once creamy white flesh. Her fair flowing hair was soon all aflame and she moved her head in a desperate attempt to shake the fire off. The blaze was consuming everything. Even her blood would drip forth from the opening skin, harden with the heat and burn. As the flesh melted from her crackling bones, her eyes grew sickeningly wider and rolled aimlessly in their deep sockets. One could hear her fearful groans and her misfortune touched everyone with a feeling of sorrow for her. Luisa's darkened skeleton could at times be seen. As the people cowered in their homes late that endless night, they could still hear her pleading for her children. They asked,

"Why should she accuse anyone of taking her beloved children from her? Did she not murder them herself?"

Her fearful lament only grew louder,

"Would she never die?"

Suddenly voices began shouting as people ran in a mad dash of confusion. Men and women alike ran inquisitively from their homes in an aimless rush of bewilderment. A distant area of the vast city was engulfed in raging orange flames which were elevated in the night air. Everyone panicked in their desperate desire to suppress the uncontrolled fire. They pushed and trampled those that were weaker and had fallen to the heated ground. Some yelled out as they neared the inflamed viceroy's palace. Several were screaming from within. As they looked in through the crystal windows of the burning rooms, they could see those inside were beyond hope of being saved. An unearthly woman in the midst of the blazing fire somehow appeared not to be burning, but moved agonizingly about the skyward flames. Luisa's eerie, piercing cry made them turn in distress to see that the executioner's pyre in the town square was still burning furiously.

Her sobbing was unceasing. They mumbled,
"La mujer llorona no para (the crying woman does not stop)!"

Soon she was called La Llorona by all as they spoke of the wailing Luisa. The following morning a large gathering went out to see La Llorona's remains. Mysteriously they found none. Several skeletal remains were found among the ashes of the burned building near the palace. Soon everyone knew from the story told by a male servant that all of the members of the Velasco and Mendoza families had perished. It was learned that Luisa's return from the dead could have caused the vengeful fire. News spread quickly throughout the terrorized city and the outlying settlements that a witch had been burned at the stake. Her damned spirit returned to cause the deaths of others.

The tragic evening of Luisa's painful execution had been disregarded by the Mendoza and Velasco families. They had gathered to enjoy a late dinner. An entertaining musician played the harpsichord and sang loudly. Not even Luisa's piercing wail could be heard. The count and viceroy toasted each others good health and forthcoming marriage of their daughter and son. Juan had apparently drank too much for he sat to one corner talking incoherently. Doña Teresa and Maria Dolores were making careful plans for the November wedding when they noticed an odor of burnt ashes enter the mysteriously darkened room. Suddenly the rattling door blew open. They began to scream hysterically when a rolling ball of fire appeared at the distant entrance.

Within the intense fire was Luisa. She was once again as a whole body, emitting a strange glow as her crying echoed throughout the room. She was dead, but yet alive.

The poor, poor child was condemned by fate. No mortal woman could have suffered more, yet her bloody murderous hands took the lives of her children. They now beheld her accursed spirit. No pity for Luisa would suffice for she was doomed to suffer an eternal misery in the fires of Hell.

Doña Teresa and Maria Dolores fainted from fright as Luisa moved towards them. The viceroy and count screamed for Juan to help them with Doña Teresa and Maria. Juan had fallen asleep and, as Luisa stood near him crying, he was surrounded by spreading flames. Luisa's pleading could be heard,

"My children, where are my children? Please give me back my children!"

Everything in the gloom filled room began to burn furiously.

One of the male servants standing near the rear door on the opposite side of the room escaped in panic. He ran until he collapsed onto the ground from shear exhaustion. Raising his unbalanced head he looked back to see the conflagration. Horrified bystanders raced to help him. He pulled his hands to his face as if to hide from his sight the shocking nightmare he had just gone through. His young wife, who worked as a chamber maid for Doña Teresa, perished when she jumped from a second floor window rather than be burned to death. A few days after telling his disheartening story, the servant killed himself.

Luisa's mournful wail could be heard late at night long after the dreadful event occurred. Those who went out after dark would return home thoroughly frightened from hearing her and having thought she was near.

The duenna herself had gone into hiding after being banished from the city by the viceroy. But rather than leave the city, she sought refuge at the convent and dedicated the rest of her painfilled life to working with the nuns. Even after the deaths of the Mendoza and Velasco families she failed to tell what she knew for fear of being named an accomplice and condemned to death.

The priest had continued listening attentively to the elderly woman as she concluded her final confession. She then admitted to the astounded priest,

"My name is Josefa Reynosa de Tablido, duenna of Luisa Gertrudis de Panuelo. I felt Luisa's true story should be revealed before my death. Other mysterious deaths have been attributed to her returning spirit."

The dumbfounded priest ended the account in his diary with,

"It is now known the tormented spirit of
Luisa Gertrudis de Panuelo, La Llorona, is
searching for her departed children. I have
given her duenna absolution and sincerely
pray that this nightmare will soon end."

Ricardo read on but did not find any other entries which
referred to La Llorona, or the elderly woman. The words on
the last written page, however, caught his attention. The
notations were begun as before, with the date and time of entry. It was two o'clock in the morning. The opening lines
read,

"I have gone through yet another sleepless
night."

His handwriting changed on this page as if writing hurriedly.

"It happened again, she appeared to me. I
fear I cannot take much more. I realize I do
not have much time left. Where could the
children have been taken? I am . . ."

For some strange unknown reason, the priest had failed to
complete his sentence. Only scribbled pen marks followed.
This bothered Ricardo as he examined the following blank
pages.

Ricardo now knew the incredible story. He, however, still
did not know the answer to end his disastrous misery. How
could he help Luisa find the resting place of her lost children
and finally peace? As Ricardo sat there looking through the
ancient diary, he could conjure up images of Luisa's death
and frightening reappearances. The flickering light coming
from the damaged lantern created moving shadows on the
ruined walls. He envisioned the merciless tribunal sitting in
judgement and all the other scenes that made up La
Llorona's tragic life. Ricardo's morbid thoughts were interrupted as he heard unfamiliar noises coming from beyond the
outer walls of the condemned church.

The strong odor of burning cinders reached his sensitive
nostrils. He glanced at the emptying lantern. It was not coming from there. The small vestry was suddenly plunged into
an eternal darkness. There was a deathly silence that filled the
tomblike chamber. Ricardo, sensing the emminent danger
that was approaching, realized it was fruitless to try to
escape. After an everlasting moment of silence a side of the

narrow room erupted in a furious ball of flames. A distorted form in the midst of the flames took a human shape. Two outstretched arms reached out for Ricardo. He could hear the agonizing moaning wail of La Llorona. The broken man was utterly filled with horror. He stood defenseless as the all consuming fire encircled him, passing into a grayish darkness as the fetid smoke thickened in the confined vestry.

Ricardo reawakened believing he had passed onto another life. Turning his giddy head rapidly about he stared with blurred eyes as he made out the strange forms in the brightening room. The friars of San Sebastian were whispering. He asked,

"Where am I?"

He was now unsure of what had happened. Was it real or imaginary? He cried out,

"How did I get here?"

Fray Alonso quickly answered,

"You were rescued from a fire which destroyed the San Geronimo mission church. You most certainly would have perished. We attempted to warn you beforehand, but you would not listen. You were apparently struck by a collapsing beam and your lantern spilled its contents onto the floor starting the fire."

Everything was seemingly answered. But then the fray remarked,

"We are sorry we could not save the poor woman who was with you! Who was she?"

"No one was with me. What woman are you talking about?"

Ricardo asked. The baffled fray looked at Ricardo strangely. But his look quickly changed to one of understanding,

"Ricardo you have been through quite an ordeal. You have not yet recovered and cannot remember what happened. Now that the mission is destroyed, perhaps you will take care of yourself and stop this irrational obsession of searching for information that does not exist."

Ricardo asked,

"What happened to the woman?"

"The old woman was pleading for help but we were unable to reach her. Her eyes were filled with terror. We called her. She began to cry. As we walked toward her she moved back deeper into the flames until we could no longer reach her. We pulled you out of the burning church. We did not know if you were still alive. The fire was finally put out, but there is not much left of the church. We searched for the woman's remains, but did not find any."

The priest's eyes were filled with tears. The appearance of the burning woman's tortured face would remain in his memory. Fray Alonso could not understand why she had not wanted to be saved.

Ricardo spoke,

"She was Luisa Gertrudis de Panuelo."

Fray Alonso seemed puzzled. He knew he had heard the name before but could not remember when or why. Deep inside he felt such sorrow. The priest asked,

"Where was the woman from?"

The distressed man could not answer. He recalled the words,

"Beware the presence of La Llorona if you dare to read her story."

If there was a curse in knowing her story, he did not want to cause any more deaths. He could not endanger the lives of the friars by telling them what he knew. He answered,

"I do not know where she was from. The old woman was at the church when I arrived there."

Weeks passed and Ricardo's health improved. He began to laugh once more. The frightening ordeal was apparently over. He was free. He was happy. No more probing questions were asked about the illusive woman who had died in the destructive flames. Ricardo's ardent desire to return to his beloved home grew stronger. He began to feel there would be no danger to his endeared family. After all he was well. La Llorona had not returned. Had knowing her strange story been the answer? He discussed his immediate plans of leaving with Fray Alonso as they strolled through the delightful gardens of the extensive monastary.

Spring had finally arrived. The flower filled gardens were wonderfully aromatic. The cheerful birds chirped pleasantly in the stately trees. Coming to an impressive monument stone, Fray Alonso stopped in silent prayer. Ricardo's expression changed as he read the archaic inscription on the memorial stone.

> "Josefa Reynosa de Tablido, Duenna of Luisa Gertrudis de Panuelo, May God have mercy on her wandering soul, for I have known her and cried with her. I have through the years gone into blackest mourning. Help me pray for her."

> "Ricardo, I do not wish to bring back the terrible experience you suffered, but I must. What was the woman's name?"

Ricardo could not forget the warning, "The curse". Was it starting over again. He fought to forget the horrible experience. He answered,

> "I do not remember."

Fray Alonso stopped his questioning. He knew Ricardo did not wish to answer. The elder fray turned as someone called him. It was time for dinner. The afflicted, young man was relieved. Realizing the priest would be concerned, he sought to hide his inner struggle. He turned to the fray as he forced a smile,

> "Come, let us eat."

Conversation at the dinner table was pleasant. The friar did not persist in his questioning. Ricardo informed the other priests,

> "It saddens me to say, I will be leaving here tomorrow. I will miss your company. You have been very gracious and considerate. But it is time for me to return to my family. I have written to them and my parents are anxious for me to return. A large caravan destined for Santa Fe will be leaving tomorrow. I will not be traveling alone."

Ricardo Valdez had a peaceful night's rest. Early the next

morning he was ready to leave. He bid the compassionate friars farewell.

Later that afternoon, Fray Alonso walked into the comfortable room Valdez had been staying in. On the small table next to his bed was an old book. He had never seen Ricardo with it. Had he brought it with him and left it behind? The brittle cover was badly burned. The inquisitive friar carefully opened it and began to read,

"Late on a moonlit night, I was awakened by hard rapping at the rectory doors. Upon opening them I found an aged, humped woman asking for sanctuary from the bitter cold. She was dressed in black and her wide shawl covered all of her wrinkled face except for her peering, penetrating eyes . . ."

He stopped reading as he thought to himself,

"The diary! It must be the diary he was looking for. He must have wanted us to keep it."

Who had placed the diary there? Would the friars be La Llorona's next victims?

After an uneventful journey, Ricardo Valdez arrived at the old capital of Santa Fe. The clear weather had been very kind and pleasureable to the contented travelers. Ricardo went directly to the adobe home of his awaiting parents. Arriving at home, Ricardo danced into the kitchen complementing his mother on how delicious the chile smelled. She was cooking his favorite meal, what more could he ask for. The happy family laughed as they sat at the dinner table. All were apparently back to normal except for his mother who tried to hide her feelings of concern for her elder son. They were overjoyed with his presence especially after such a long absence. He looked well and he felt well.

That evening the devoted son sat conversing with his family. They inquired about La Llorona and what he had learned. He would not say. They insisted on knowing. He surprised them by answering angrily,

"I cannot tell you. It is better that you do not know. I am well now. There is no need to ever bring the subject up again!"

His surprised family agreed. Ricardo's well being was their

93

prime concern. Exhausted with the trying day, the weary man decided to retire early. He went to pull down the full covers of his soft feather bed. He suddenly jumped back horrified. The cruel scythe which the Angel of Death had held in the vestry of the church of San Geronimo lay there bloodstained. Wording engraved on the admonishing blade proclaimed the futility of his endless struggle,

"If you gaze upon her tormented face, she will live with you for the rest of your earthly life."

www.ingramcontent.com/pod-product-compliance
Lightning Source LLC
Chambersburg PA
CBHW031216270326
41931CB00006B/585